THE
WISDOM
WALK

THE WISDOM WALK

31 DAYS IN THE BOOK OF PROVERBS

GEORGE BLOOMER

W

WHITAKER
HOUSE

Unless otherwise indicated, all Scripture quotations are taken from the King James Version of the Holy Bible.

Wisdom Walk:
31 Days in the Book of Proverbs

For speaking engagements, you may contact the author at:
Blooming House Publishers / Bethel Family Worship Center
515 Dowd Street
Durham, NC 27701
www.bethelfamily.org

ISBN: 978-1-60374-437-9
Printed in the United States of America
© 2005, 2012 by George Bloomer

Whitaker House
1030 Hunt Valley Circle
New Kensington, PA 15068
www.whitakerhouse.com

This book has been printed digitally and produced in a standard specification in order to ensure its continuing availability.

Introduction:
Wisdom Thoughts I Couldn't Do Without

The book of Proverbs is loaded with the poetic illustrations of wisdom's invaluable assets to mankind.

> *For wisdom is better than rubies; and all the things that may be desired are not to be compared to it.* (Proverbs 8:11)

It continually drives home the necessity of wisdom as it relates to our daily experiences, and to our walk with God. Proverbs encompasses the supernatural insight that He blesses us with in order to make the proper decisions in life, and to remain on the most direct path toward our God-ordained destinies.

The objective of this book is to whisper a gentle reminder that you should never discount life's lessons, regardless of how great or small. Nothing in life is an accident. In all things, there is purpose. And while we don't always see the full picture of what is about to take place in our lives, God the Father allows us to see glimpses of the future, and gives us instructions in phases on how to arrive at each destination. This is the wisdom of God in operation.

Wisdom and understanding are vital components to the life of the believer, and the lifesaving ingredients that sustain us from the snares and entrapments that seek to steal our destiny. In all matters, *"wisdom is the principal thing"* (Proverbs 4:7). Whether it has to do with your family, finances, or mental and emotional well-being, the wisdom of God is an applicable component to right decision making and in maintaining the integrity of your godly stand.

All too often, the word *wisdom* is loosely defined as a means of comparing mankind's carnal intellect to God's all-knowing power. Daily, without us being fully aware of it, the Lord fills us up with

His many benefits through divine knowledge, guidance, and inspiration. God's supernatural ability working through the life of the believer is evident in our daily accomplishments—acts that may seem like impossible feats without His hand leading and guiding us.

The book of Proverbs sites practical principles to enlighten our understanding of this divine guidance with its many lessons on family, finances, integrity, respect for mankind, and the fear of the Lord. In the midst of making difficult decisions, it's the wisdom of God that stands as our proxy, giving our mouths the right words to say, and leading our feet in the direction that we should go. *"For the LORD giveth wisdom: out of his mouth cometh knowledge and understanding"* (Proverbs 2:6).

Thinking on things that are honest, just, pure, lovely, and of good report rejuvenates and fortifies your wisdom.

> *Finally, brethren, whatsoever things are true, whatsoever things are honest, whatsoever things are just, whatsoever things are pure, whatsoever things are lovely, whatsoever things are of good report; if there be any virtue, and if there be any praise, think on these things.* (Philippians 4:8)

In hindsight, I can recall that, even at a young age, God was sprinkling His gift of supernatural wisdom and understanding upon me, to preserve my mind, renew my spirit, and to prepare me for such a time as this.

It's October 30, 1972, at P. S. 27, my school in New York City. A nine-year-old boy sits on the steps at 6:00 a.m., waiting for the building to open. He has no books, no crayons, no pencils, no pens. He sits in the clothes that he wore the day before and slept in last night. He's hungry; his last meal was noon yesterday. It's cold on this day before Halloween. That's what keeps him going—Halloween, his favorite holiday—the day he gets to dress up, and, for a moment, become whomever he decides to be. And on that day, he decides to become the brainless scarecrow from *The Wizard of Oz*.

He can't see his future for his present state of mind, and this place of learning has become a place of survival. It's where he gets to eat breakfast and lunch, and see friends. Nonetheless, it's also a place where he isn't able to learn. He is the seventh of ten children, another number in the welfare system. Little does he know what lies in store for him in life. Prison, sexual abuse, and addiction will all come knocking in an attempt to seal the deal to his fate. Today, he's in the fourth grade. In five more years, he'll be in the ninth grade of another school, but, intellectually, he'll be no smarter than he is this day in the fourth grade.

He has been labeled a "problem child," incapable of learning, and tossed into a special needs class for CEH students (Certified Emotionally Handicapped). Without mentors or positive role models in his environment, he begins to conform into the person that others forecast him to become. He takes his daily dose of Ritalin, as prescribed by those who gave a stamp of approval to his incorrigible plight. No one can see that his problems are not due to irreparable mental damage. It's the hunger pains that interrupt his concentration. It's the lack of positive role models that force him to produce his own self-image. It's the hand-me-down clothes that provoke the taunting from peers, causing him to lash out in anger or act out in absurdity.

When your mother and father forsake you, it is the Lord who will take you up. What school did not, or could not, teach him, divine intervention and godly wisdom did. God became preoccupied with him, giving him wisdom to make up for this lack of knowledge. And for this wisdom, the young boy gave God praise. And for such praise, God gave him intelligence. No, this boy was not smart by formal educational standards, but he was unusually wise.

This is why Philippians 4:13 reminds us of our supernatural abilities, through Jesus Christ, to sustain all things. *"I can do all things through Christ which strengtheneth me."* Regardless of your present situation, you have been endowed with power from on high to handle the pressures of life, as God gives you supernatural vision to tunnel through them and arise with victory. When the hand of God is upon your life, He will not allow you to hide behind the clueless decisions of a brainless scarecrow. Instead, He will use those things that were intended to scare others off as a vessel to draw men and women to Christ.

The irony of my choice of costume during Halloween was that, despite an infinite array of possibilities, my finite imagination chose a character who could not think for himself, who had no brain, and who was clumsy and awkward in stature.

Amazingly, my choice of costume would mirror some of the bad choices I made later in life. Still, in His infinite wisdom, God knew everything about me, things that my present situation had not yet revealed. He knew that, one day, I would be used by Him as a mighty force to set others free from the same yokes of bondage that I was enduring at that time. Because the hand of the Lord was on my life, He supernaturally endowed me with wisdom that far exceeded my years of knowledge and understanding—wisdom that would override the brainless scarecrow syndrome that the devil desired for me. I was walking a tightrope of stupidity, but when I lost my balance, I fell into a net of wisdom that God had placed beneath me. Without that net, my falls of stupidity would have fatally wounded me.

Take a moment to meditate on the things the devil has taken from you, and ask God to restore them, with interest. (See 1Samuel 30.)

I pray that, as you record your personal thoughts in this book, the wisdom of God will overtake you, giving you supernatural insight and ability to accomplish impossible feats. Let's walk with God together for thirty-one days. Let's journey to a place that will change our lives forever. Can't you hear God saying, "Come, walk with Me"?

Wisdom Talks

Scripture says, *"If thou shalt confess with thy mouth the Lord Jesus, and shalt believe in thine heart that God hath raised him from the dead, thou shalt be saved"* (Romans 10:9). In implementing the Word of the Lord as a viable component within your daily walk with Him, you must combine the ability to listen to His instructions with a willingness to speak according to His commands. Wisdom is *"swift to hear, slow to speak, slow to wrath"* (James 1:19). When you're coming for wisdom, you do not come only with lips, but with ears, also.

"Death and life are in the power of the tongue" (Proverbs 18:21). The words you speak have the capacity to make a bad situation worse, or to provoke a miracle from heaven on your behalf. *"If ye shall say unto this mountain, be thou removed, and be thou cast into the sea; it shall be done"* (Matthew 21:21). The act of speaking triggers action in the Spirit world. Wisdom is the principle thing. So, if we're going to think and walk in wisdom, we must ask God to help us speak things that are pure and correct.

Wisdom is like shelter during a storm. It is being rescued from a fire. It is the inner voice given by God in the midst of crises, helping you to execute a way of escape. Those who have the gift of wisdom are never so distracted by the beauty and architecture of a building that they fail to notice the exits. Wisdom teaches you how to plan your exit.

On an airplane, you're given the proper instructions on how to escape in case of a malfunction, increasing your chances of survival if catastrophic failure occurs. The flight attendants point out the exits throughout the plane, while the announcement says, "Remember, your closest exit may be behind you." Sometimes, you must go backward in order to get out. The flight attendant fore-warns you of the possibility of a loss of air pressure in the cabin, and what to do and what not to do if this happens. Adults traveling with children are to place their own masks on first before assisting the child. You also are reminded that your seat can be used as a floatation device. These safety instructions are much like wisdom, which tells you to enjoy your flight, but, in case things don't go as planned, there are alternate routes to escape life's unexpected catastrophes.

Proverbs 1

¹The proverbs of Solomon the son of David, king of Israel;
²To know wisdom and instruction; to perceive the words of understanding;
³To receive the instruction of wisdom, justice, and judgment, and equity;
⁴To give subtlety to the simple, to the young man knowledge and discretion.
⁵A wise man will hear, and will increase learning; and a man of understanding shall attain unto wise counsels:
⁶To understand a proverb, and the interpretation; the words of the wise, and their dark sayings.
⁷The fear of the Lord is the beginning of knowledge: but fools despise wisdom and instruction.
⁸My son, hear the instruction of thy father, and forsake not the law of thy mother:
⁹For they shall be an ornament of grace unto thy head, and chains about thy neck.
¹⁰My son, if sinners entice thee, consent thou not.
¹¹If they say, Come with us, let us lay wait for blood, let us lurk privily for the innocent without cause:
¹²Let us swallow them up alive as the grave; and whole, as those that go down into the pit:
¹³We shall find all precious substance, we shall fill our houses with spoil:
¹⁴Cast in thy lot among us; let us all have one purse:
¹⁵My son, walk not thou in the way with them; refrain thy foot from their path:
¹⁶For their feet run to evil, and make haste to shed blood.
¹⁷Surely in vain the net is spread in the sight of any bird.
¹⁸And they lay wait for their own blood; they lurk privily for their own lives.

¹⁹So are the ways of every one that is greedy of gain; which taketh away the life of the owners thereof.
²⁰Wisdom crieth without; she uttereth her voice in the streets:
²¹She crieth in the chief place of concourse, in the openings of the gates: in the city she uttereth her words, saying,
²²How long, ye simple ones, will ye love simplicity? and the scorners delight in their scorning, and fools hate knowledge?
²³Turn you at my reproof: behold, I will pour out my spirit unto you, I will make known my words unto you.
²⁴Because I have called, and ye refused; I have stretched out my hand, and no man regarded;
²⁵But ye have set at nought all my counsel, and would none of my reproof:
²⁶I also will laugh at your calamity; I will mock when your fear cometh;
²⁷When your fear cometh as desolation, and your destruction cometh as a whirlwind; when distress and anguish cometh upon you.
²⁸Then shall they call upon me, but I will not answer; they shall seek me early, but they shall not find me:
²⁹For that they hated knowledge, and did not choose the fear of the Lord:
³⁰They would none of my counsel: they despised all my reproof.
³¹Therefore shall they eat of the fruit of their own way, and be filled with their own devices.
³²For the turning away of the simple shall slay them, and the prosperity of fools shall destroy them.
³³But whoso hearkeneth unto me shall dwell safely, and shall be quiet from fear of evil.

Wisdom Key

Walks of wisdom are measured by the prudence of a man's character.

Today's Prayer

Father, help me to accept rebuke and instruction. Help me to receive wisdom and to cherish it as a precious and priceless gift from You. I want to be wise and discerning. I want to fear You and to walk uprightly before You. Help me to hold on to the teaching I have received from my natural and spiritual parents, so that I can live the holy, blameless life You have called me to.

Q & A with George Bloomer

What is the spiritual definition of wisdom and is it something that we're automatically given after salvation, or do we have to seek the Lord for it?

The answer is both. Wisdom is something you get when you receive the Lord. Although you already have it, you ask the Lord to stir up the gift. Wisdom is a gift, and gifts can be coveted or asked for. The word *wisdom* is defined by the dictionary as "the quality or state of being wise; knowledge of what is true or right coupled with just judgment as to action; sagacity, discernment, or insight" (Dictionary.com); or, "the knowledge and experience needed to make sensible decisions and judgments, or the good sense shown by the decisions and judgments made" (author's definition). The spiritual definition of "wisdom" doesn't veer that much from the secular definition of it. It is a window into the mind or the psyche of God. This window is an eternal window that helps you to sort out things in time and properly execute the wisdom you have already received. For instance, if you have formal knowledge from what's written in books, or the experiences of others, then you're equipped with knowledge, but you may not have the wisdom to execute the knowledge that you have. This wisdom on execution, which is godly experience or the window into the psyche of God, gives you the ability to give the God-like answer to the physical knowledge that you have, in order to make the right decisions that pertain to your life.

Today's Positive Achievement

_____

_____

_____

_____

_____

_____

_____

_____

_____

_____

_____

_____

_____

_____

_____

_____

_____

_____

_____

_____

¹My son, if thou wilt receive my words, and hide my commandments with thee; ²So that thou incline thine ear unto wisdom, and apply thine heart to understanding; ³Yea, if thou criest after knowledge, and liftest up thy voice for understanding; ⁴If thou seekest her as silver, and searchest for her as for hid treasures; ⁵Then shalt thou understand the fear of the LORD, and find the knowledge of God. ⁶For the LORD giveth wisdom: out of his mouth cometh knowledge and understanding. ⁷He layeth up sound wisdom for the righteous: he is a buckler to them that walk uprightly. ⁸He keepeth the paths of judgment, and preserveth the way of his saints. ⁹Then shalt thou understand righteousness, and judgment, and equity; yea, every good path. ¹⁰When wisdom entereth into thine heart, and knowledge is pleasant unto thy soul; ¹¹Discretion shall preserve thee, understanding shall keep thee:

¹²To deliver thee from the way of the evil man, from the man that speaketh froward things; ¹³Who leave the paths of uprightness, to walk in the ways of darkness; ¹⁴Who rejoice to do evil, and delight in the frowardness of the wicked; ¹⁵Whose ways are crooked, and they froward in their paths: ¹⁶To deliver thee from the strange woman, even from the stranger which flattereth with her words; ¹⁷Which forsaketh the guide of her youth, and forgetteth the covenant of her God. ¹⁸For her house inclineth unto death, and her paths unto the dead. ¹⁹None that go unto her return again, neither take they hold of the paths of life. ²⁰That thou mayest walk in the way of good men, and keep the paths of the righteous. ²¹For the upright shall dwell in the land, and the perfect shall remain in it. ²²But the wicked shall be cut off from the earth, and the transgressors shall be rooted out of it.

Wisdom Key

The ability to receive instruction is the open door to divine destiny.

Today's Prayer

Help me to know and understand the fear of the Lord. Turn my ear to wisdom and my heart to understanding. Help me know and understand You and Your ways. I long for Your revelation, and my heart cries out for your instruction. As I receive wisdom and learn to apply it to my life, keep me from evil and destruction.

Q & A with Bishop George Bloomer

What do I do if I have missed God and turned away from the plan and purpose He had for my life?

Ask for forgiveness and get back on His path.

Today's Positive Achievement

_____

_____

_____

_____

_____

_____

_____

_____

_____

_____

_____

_____

_____

_____

_____

_____

_____

_____

_____

_____

Proverbs 3

¹My son, forget not my law; but let thine heart keep my commandments:

²For length of days, and long life, and peace, shall they add to thee.

³Let not mercy and truth forsake thee: bind them about thy neck; write them upon the table of thine heart:

⁴So shalt thou find favour and good understanding in the sight of God and man.

⁵Trust in the LORD with all thine heart; and lean not unto thine own understanding.

⁶In all thy ways acknowledge him, and he shall direct thy paths.

⁷Be not wise in thine own eyes: fear the LORD, and depart from evil.

⁸It shall be health to thy navel, and marrow to thy bones.

⁹Honour the LORD with thy substance, and with the firstfruits of all thine increase:

¹⁰So shall thy barns be filled with plenty, and thy presses shall burst out with new wine.

¹¹My son, despise not the chastening of the LORD; neither be weary of his correction:

¹²For whom the LORD loveth he correcteth; even as a father the son in whom he delighteth.

¹³Happy is the man that findeth wisdom, and the man that getteth understanding.

¹⁴For the merchandise of it is better than the merchandise of silver, and the gain thereof than fine gold.

¹⁵She is more precious than rubies: and all the things thou canst desire are not to be compared unto her.

¹⁶Length of days is in her right hand; and in her left hand riches and honour.

¹⁷Her ways are ways of pleasantness, and all her paths are peace.

¹⁸She is a tree of life to them that lay hold upon her: and happy is every one that retaineth her.

¹⁹The LORD by wisdom hath founded the earth; by understanding hath he established the heavens.

²⁰By his knowledge the depths are broken up, and the clouds drop down the dew.

²¹My son, let not them depart from thine eyes: keep sound wisdom and discretion:

²²So shall they be life unto thy soul, and grace to thy neck.

²³Then shalt thou walk in thy way safely, and thy foot shall not stumble.

²⁴When thou liest down, thou shalt not be afraid: yea, thou shalt lie down, and thy sleep shall be sweet.

²⁵Be not afraid of sudden fear, neither of the desolation of the wicked, when it cometh.

²⁶For the LORD shall be thy confidence, and shall keep thy foot from being taken.

²⁷Withhold not good from them to whom it is due, when it is in the power of thine hand to do it.

²⁸Say not unto thy neighbour, Go, and come again, and to morrow I will give; when thou hast it by thee.

²⁹Devise not evil against thy neighbour, seeing he dwelleth securely by thee.

³⁰Strive not with a man without cause, if he have done thee no harm.

³¹Envy thou not the oppressor, and choose none of his ways.

³²For the froward is abomination to the LORD: but his secret is with the righteous.

³³The curse of the LORD is in the house of the wicked: but he blesseth the habitation of the just.

³⁴Surely he scorneth the scorners: but he giveth grace unto the lowly.

³⁵The wise shall inherit glory: but shame shall be the promotion of fools.

Wisdom Key

Seek the Lord in all things and repel the wisdom of fools.

Today's Prayer

Lord, Jesus, I want my life to be a living Bible for others to read. Help me to welcome wisdom into every facet of my life and show me how to pass the insight I receive on to the generations that come after me. As I embrace wisdom, show me how to hear and obey Your instructions.

Q & A with Bishop George Bloomer

How do parents teach children to become wise adults?

By example, by being a wise adult, and by subtle teachings. Parents can also use subtle principles that children can gravitate to, such as chats on the way to school. Seize every opportunity to drop "wisdom nuggets," encouraging children by reminding them of how intelligent they are and continuing to build their confidence. Confidence ultimately teaches them lessons on wisdom.

Today's Positive Achievement

_____

_____

_____

_____

_____

_____

_____

_____

_____

_____

_____

_____

_____

_____

_____

_____

_____

_____

Day Four

Proverbs 4

¹Hear, ye children, the instruction of a father, and attend to know understanding. ²For I give you good doctrine, forsake ye not my law. ³For I was my father's son, tender and only beloved in the sight of my mother. ⁴He taught me also, and said unto me, Let thine heart retain my words: keep my commandments, and live. ⁵Get wisdom, get understanding: forget it not; neither decline from the words of my mouth. ⁶Forsake her not, and she shall preserve thee: love her, and she shall keep thee. ⁷Wisdom is the principal thing; therefore get wisdom: and with all thy getting get understanding. ⁸Exalt her, and she shall promote thee: she shall bring thee to honour, when thou dost embrace her. ⁹She shall give to thine head an ornament of grace: a crown of glory shall she deliver to thee. ¹⁰Hear, O my son, and receive my sayings; and the years of thy life shall be many. ¹¹I have taught thee in the way of wisdom; I have led thee in right paths. ¹²When thou goest, thy steps shall not be straitened; and when thou runnest, thou shalt not stumble.

¹³Take fast hold of instruction; let her not go: keep her; for she is thy life. ¹⁴Enter not into the path of the wicked, and go not in the way of evil men. ¹⁵Avoid it, pass not by it, turn from it, and pass away. ¹⁶For they sleep not, except they have done mischief; and their sleep is taken away, unless they cause some to fall. ¹⁷For they eat the bread of wickedness, and drink the wine of violence. ¹⁸But the path of the just is as the shining light, that shineth more and more unto the perfect day. ¹⁹The way of the wicked is as darkness: they know not at what they stumble. ²⁰My son, attend to my words; incline thine ear unto my sayings. ²¹Let them not depart from thine eyes; keep them in the midst of thine heart. ²²For they are life unto those that find them, and health to all their flesh. ²³Keep thy heart with all diligence; for out of it are the issues of life. ²⁴Put away from thee a froward mouth, and perverse lips put far from thee. ²⁵Let thine eyes look right on, and let thine eyelids look straight before thee. ²⁶Ponder the path of thy feet, and let all thy ways be established. ²⁷Turn not to the right hand nor to the left: remove thy foot from evil.

Wisdom Key

Personal experiences are the best tutors. Never cease to learn
from the valuable lessons that they teach.

Today's Prayer

Father, what is the difference between wisdom and understanding? Help me to gain both together so that I will be able to apply the principles I have gained. Show me the way to understanding. Direct my life and order my steps so that I can follow the narrow path that leads to a life lived in Your presence.

Q & A with Bishop George Bloomer

Without the proper mentorship as a youth, how does a man or woman go on in life to be a productive adult who makes a positive impact in society?

Unfortunately, many times they don't, and this is why social workers and the Big Brother/Big Sister programs are so important—to mentor and guide those who lack the proper mentorship in their youth, helping to steer them onto the right path. I didn't have any mentors. I didn't have anyone to help cultivate or shape me. The Bible teaches that when mother and father forsake you, then the Lord will take you up. (See Psalm 27:10.) When God becomes preoccupied with you, He has a way of quantum-leaping your life and carrying you back into your childhood as an adult in order to develop and mature you. It is a spiritual reformation that takes place and has taken place in the lives of many adults who did not receive the mentorship when they were young, but are still able to maintain a productive and wholesome lifestyle as adults.

Today's Positive Achievement

_____

_____

_____

_____

_____

_____

_____

_____

_____

_____

_____

_____

_____

_____

_____

_____

_____

_____

_____

Day Five

Proverbs 5

¹My son, attend unto my wisdom, and bow thine ear to my understanding: ²That thou mayest regard discretion, and that thy lips may keep knowledge. ³For the lips of a strange woman drop as an honeycomb, and her mouth is smoother than oil: ⁴But her end is bitter as wormwood, sharp as a two-edged sword. ⁵Her feet go down to death; her steps take hold on hell. ⁶Lest thou shouldest ponder the path of life, her ways are moveable, that thou canst not know them. ⁷Hear me now therefore, O ye children, and depart not from the words of my mouth. ⁸Remove thy way far from her, and come not nigh the door of her house: ⁹Lest thou give thine honour unto others, and thy years unto the cruel: ¹⁰Lest strangers be filled with thy wealth; and thy labours be in the house of a stranger; ¹¹And thou mourn at the last, when thy flesh and thy body are consumed, ¹²And say, How have I hated instruction, and my heart despised reproof;

¹³And have not obeyed the voice of my teachers, nor inclined mine ear to them that instructed me! ¹⁴I was almost in all evil in the midst of the congregation and assembly. ¹⁵Drink waters out of thine own cistern, and running waters out of thine own well. ¹⁶Let thy fountains be dispersed abroad, and rivers of waters in the streets. ¹⁷Let them be only thine own, and not strangers' with thee. ¹⁸Let thy fountain be blessed: and rejoice with the wife of thy youth. ¹⁹Let her be as the loving hind and pleasant roe; let her breasts satisfy thee at all times; and be thou ravished always with her love. ²⁰And why wilt thou, my son, be ravished with a strange woman, and embrace the bosom of a stranger? ²¹For the ways of man are before the eyes of the Lord, and he pondereth all his goings. ²²His own iniquities shall take the wicked himself, and he shall be holden with the cords of his sins. ²³He shall die without instruction; and in the greatness of his folly he shall go astray.

Wisdom Key

Managing one's own home with godly wisdom unlocks the door to God's blessings and invokes His hand of mercy and grace.

Today's Prayer

Fortify my home, Father, and strengthen the divine relationships that You have ordained in my life. Guide me as I throw off the weights and obstacles of perilous relationships. Cover me in Your love so I can focus my mind on things that are pure and concentrate on ministering to You.

Q & A with Bishop George Bloomer

When the fear of being alone, unloved, and rejected causes you to compromise your morals and integrity, how do you ask God for forgiveness and get out of an ungodly relationship when you've already fallen deeply in love?

The middle part of the question is "How do you ask God for forgiveness?" You ask God for forgiveness by simply asking Him for forgiveness. There is no structured teaching for asking God's forgiveness. A broken heart and a contrite spirit, God will not despise. (See Psalm 51:17.) Many times, when we deal with loneliness, and rejection, the feelings of insecurity due to not being loved and covered sometimes produce strong lust that fills our areas of lack. If you're feeling convicted, then the battle now is not that you do not understand that it is wrong. The battle is that you know that it is wrong, but at the same time, you're hooked. Go to God and ask Him for His help to set you free from this ungodly situation. Like any other addiction, cold turkey normally works.

Today's Positive Achievement

Day Six

Proverbs 6

¹My son, if thou be surety for thy friend, if thou hast stricken thy hand with a stranger,
²Thou art snared with the words of thy mouth, thou art taken with the words of thy mouth.
³Do this now, my son, and deliver thyself, when thou art come into the hand of thy friend; go, humble thyself, and make sure thy friend.
⁴Give not sleep to thine eyes, nor slumber to thine eyelids.
⁵Deliver thyself as a roe from the hand of the hunter, and as a bird from the hand of the fowler.
⁶Go to the ant, thou sluggard; consider her ways, and be wise:
⁷Which having no guide, overseer, or ruler,
⁸Provideth her meat in the summer, and gathereth her food in the harvest.
⁹How long wilt thou sleep, O sluggard? when wilt thou arise out of thy sleep?
¹⁰Yet a little sleep, a little slumber, a little folding of the hands to sleep:
¹¹So shall thy poverty come as one that travelleth, and thy want as an armed man.
¹²A naughty person, a wicked man, walketh with a froward mouth.
¹³He winketh with his eyes, he speaketh with his feet, he teacheth with his fingers;
¹⁴Frowardness is in his heart, he deviseth mischief continually; he soweth discord.
¹⁵Therefore shall his calamity come suddenly; suddenly shall he be broken without remedy.
¹⁶These six things doth the Lᴏʀᴅ hate: yea, seven are an abomination unto him:
¹⁷A proud look, a lying tongue, and hands that shed innocent blood,
¹⁸An heart that deviseth wicked imaginations, feet that be swift in running to mischief,

¹⁹A false witness that speaketh lies, and he that soweth discord among brethren.
²⁰My son, keep thy father's commandment, and forsake not the law of thy mother:
²¹Bind them continually upon thine heart, and tie them about thy neck.
²²When thou goest, it shall lead thee; when thou sleepest, it shall keep thee; and when thou awakest, it shall talk with thee.
²³For the commandment is a lamp; and the law is light; and reproofs of instruction are the way of life:
²⁴To keep thee from the evil woman, from the flattery of the tongue of a strange woman.
²⁵Lust not after her beauty in thine heart; neither let her take thee with her eyelids.
²⁶For by means of a whorish woman a man is brought to a piece of bread: and the adultress will hunt for the precious life.
²⁷Can a man take fire in his bosom, and his clothes not be burned?
²⁸Can one go upon hot coals, and his feet not be burned?
²⁹So he that goeth in to his neighbour's wife; whosoever toucheth her shall not be innocent.
³⁰Men do not despise a thief, if he steal to satisfy his soul when he is hungry;
³¹But if he be found, he shall restore sevenfold; he shall give all the substance of his house.
³²But whoso committeth adultery with a woman lacketh understanding: he that doeth it destroyeth his own soul.
³³A wound and dishonour shall he get; and his reproach shall not be wiped away.
³⁴For jealousy is the rage of a man: therefore he will not spare in the day of vengeance.
³⁵He will not regard any ransom; neither will he rest content, though thou givest many gifts.

Wisdom Key

Wrath and unforgiveness are the devil's psychological warfare against the mind. Go make peace with a friend or foe.

Today's Prayer

Bitterness and sin have caused a black, cancerous cyst to grow on my heart and spirit. Father, remove this disease of bitterness that has overtaken my soul. Help me to turn from sin and from the evil thoughts that flood my mind daily. Help me to drink in the fresh water of Your Word so that I can forgive and be cleansed.

Q & A with Bishop George Bloomer

After repeatedly being used by those you love, how do you overcome the bitterness and forgive without allowing yourself to continue to go through the same negative cycles?

Again, that's one of those things that takes the wisdom of God. There are some people who are hosts to anger, bitterness, envy, jealousy, and strife. They're hosts to those viruses. Then, there are others who are hosts to forgiveness, giving another chance and offering others the benefit of the doubt. You must find out what your host-ability is, what your host-womb is. A virus cannot exist without a host. Stop hosting, and the virus will stop existing.

Today's Positive Achievement

_____
_____
_____
_____
_____
_____
_____
_____
_____
_____
_____
_____
_____
_____
_____
_____
_____
_____
_____
_____
_____
_____
_____

Day Seven

Proverbs 7

¹My son, keep my words, and lay up my commandments with thee.
²Keep my commandments, and live; and my law as the apple of thine eye.
³Bind them upon thy fingers, write them upon the table of thine heart.
⁴Say unto wisdom, Thou art my sister; and call understanding thy kinswoman:
⁵That they may keep thee from the strange woman, from the stranger which flattereth with her words.
⁶For at the window of my house I looked through my casement,
⁷And beheld among the simple ones, I discerned among the youths, a young man void of understanding,
⁸Passing through the street near her corner; and he went the way to her house,
⁹In the twilight, in the evening, in the black and dark night:
¹⁰And, behold, there met him a woman with the attire of an harlot, and subtil of heart.
¹¹(She is loud and stubborn; her feet abide not in her house:
¹²Now is she without, now in the streets, and lieth in wait at every corner.)
¹³So she caught him, and kissed him, and with an impudent face said unto him,
¹⁴I have peace offerings with me; this day have I payed my vows.
¹⁵Therefore came I forth to meet thee, diligently to seek thy face, and I have found thee.
¹⁶I have decked my bed with coverings of tapestry, with carved works, with fine linen of Egypt.
¹⁷I have perfumed my bed with myrrh, aloes, and cinnamon.
¹⁸Come, let us take our fill of love until the morning: let us solace ourselves with loves.
¹⁹For the goodman is not at home, he is gone a long journey:
²⁰He hath taken a bag of money with him, and will come home at the day appointed.
²¹With her much fair speech she caused him to yield, with the flattering of her lips she forced him.
²²He goeth after her straightway, as an ox goeth to the slaughter, or as a fool to the correction of the stocks;
²³Till a dart strike through his liver; as a bird hasteth to the snare, and knoweth not that it is for his life.
²⁴Hearken unto me now therefore, O ye children, and attend to the words of my mouth.
²⁵Let not thine heart decline to her ways, go not astray in her paths.
²⁶For she hath cast down many wounded: yea, many strong men have been slain by her.
²⁷Her house is the way to hell, going down to the chambers of death.

Wisdom Key

Don't be enticed by the subtle tactics of Satan's deceit. He is a snare unto your feet that darkens the path toward your divine walk of destiny.

Today's Prayer

Father, keep me from being seduced by tempting words and lying tongues. Help my intellect and discernment to be alert at all times as I encounter people and situations that threaten to lead me away from the destiny You have purposed for my life. Orchestrate divine appointments and connections for me daily and help me to walk in a way that generates peace everywhere my feet tread.

Q & A with Bishop George Bloomer

In seeking a permanent mate, what qualities should permeate as rigid requirements?

Permanency in the finite world of time means forever. When picking a forever and ever partner, you must take enough time to know what your forever needs are going to be. Therefore, you must sit down and consider the cost of permanency. This is not a temporary location. This is not a temporary mate. This is a permanent mate. So, in order for you to dwell with the self esteem, personal growth, and the sense of personal and self accomplishments, to feel secure, you must tell yourself, "I need this, this, and that." Get a piece of paper and write down your "this and that," and know that those are the things that you'll need and stick to it. By doing this before you enter a committed relationship, you heighten your chances of finding the right mate—that is *if* you stick to your "this, this, this, and that." Additionally, your potential mate being saved won't hurt; and his or her loving the Lord like you do probably won't hurt, either.

Today's Positive Achievement

Day Eight
Proverbs 8

¹Doth not wisdom cry? and understanding put forth her voice?
²She standeth in the top of high places, by the way in the places of the paths.
³She crieth at the gates, at the entry of the city, at the coming in at the doors.
⁴Unto you, O men, I call; and my voice is to the sons of man.
⁵O ye simple, understand wisdom: and, ye fools, be ye of an understanding heart.
⁶Hear; for I will speak of excellent things; and the opening of my lips shall be right things.
⁷For my mouth shall speak truth; and wickedness is an abomination to my lips.
⁸All the words of my mouth are in righteousness; there is nothing froward or perverse in them.
⁹They are all plain to him that understandeth, and right to them that find knowledge.
¹⁰Receive my instruction, and not silver; and knowledge rather than choice gold.
¹¹For wisdom is better than rubies; and all the things that may be desired are not to be compared to it.
¹²I wisdom dwell with prudence, and find out knowledge of witty inventions.
¹³The fear of the Lord is to hate evil: pride, and arrogancy, and the evil way, and the froward mouth, do I hate.
¹⁴Counsel is mine, and sound wisdom: I am understanding; I have strength.
¹⁵By me kings reign, and princes decree justice.
¹⁶By me princes rule, and nobles, even all the judges of the earth.
¹⁷I love them that love me; and those that seek me early shall find me.
¹⁸Riches and honour are with me; yea, durable riches and righteousness.
¹⁹My fruit is better than gold, yea, than fine gold; and my revenue than choice silver.
²⁰I lead in the way of righteousness, in the midst of the paths of judgment:
²¹That I may cause those that love me to inherit substance; and I will fill their treasures.
²²The Lord possessed me in the beginning of his way, before his works of old.
²³I was set up from everlasting, from the beginning, or ever the earth was.
²⁴When there were no depths, I was brought forth; when there were no fountains abounding with water.
²⁵Before the mountains were settled, before the hills was I brought forth:
²⁶While as yet he had not made the earth, nor the fields, nor the highest part of the dust of the world.
²⁷When he prepared the heavens, I was there: when he set a compass upon the face of the depth:
²⁸When he established the clouds above: when he strengthened the fountains of the deep:
²⁹When he gave to the sea his decree, that the waters should not pass his commandment: when he appointed the foundations of the earth:
³⁰Then I was by him, as one brought up with him: and I was daily his delight, rejoicing always before him;
³¹Rejoicing in the habitable part of his earth; and my delights were with the sons of men.
³²Now therefore hearken unto me, O ye children: for blessed are they that keep my ways.
³³Hear instruction, and be wise, and refuse it not.
³⁴Blessed is the man that heareth me, watching daily at my gates, waiting at the posts of my doors.
³⁵For whoso findeth me findeth life, and shall obtain favour of the Lord.
³⁶But he that sinneth against me wrongeth his own soul: all they that hate me love death.

Wisdom Key

To fear the Lord is to love Him, and to love Him is to embrace eternal life. Get to know God better.

Today's Prayer

God, even You required the assistance of wisdom as You created the earth. How much more, then, do I need the help of wisdom and discretion each day to succeed in this life? I pray that wisdom becomes my counselor as I try to walk along the path of righteousness.

Q & A with Bishop George Bloomer

When ungodly counsel has caused havoc to take place in your life, how can you dig through the repercussions of bad decision making to get on the right track toward wise decision making?

Admit to yourself that your counsel was wrong. Start all over again. This does not take rocket-science.

Today's Positive Achievement

_____

_____

_____

_____

_____

_____

_____

_____

_____

_____

_____

_____

_____

_____

_____

_____

_____

_____

_____

_____

_____

_____

_____

Proverbs 9

[1]Wisdom hath builded her house, she hath hewn out her seven pillars:

[2]She hath killed her beasts; she hath mingled her wine; she hath also furnished her table.

[3]She hath sent forth her maidens: she crieth upon the highest places of the city,

[4]Whoso is simple, let him turn in hither: as for him that wanteth understanding, she saith to him,

[5]Come, eat of my bread, and drink of the wine which I have mingled.

[6]Forsake the foolish, and live; and go in the way of understanding.

[7]He that reproveth a scorner getteth to himself shame: and he that rebuketh a wicked man getteth himself a blot.

[8]Reprove not a scorner, lest he hate thee: rebuke a wise man, and he will love thee.

[9]Give instruction to a wise man, and he will be yet wiser: teach a just man, and he will increase in learning.

[10]The fear of the LORD is the beginning of wisdom: and the knowledge of the holy is understanding.

[11]For by me thy days shall be multiplied, and the years of thy life shall be increased.

[12]If thou be wise, thou shalt be wise for thyself: but if thou scornest, thou alone shalt bear it.

[13]A foolish woman is clamorous: she is simple, and knoweth nothing.

[14]For she sitteth at the door of her house, on a seat in the high places of the city,

[15]To call passengers who go right on their ways:

[16]Whoso is simple, let him turn in hither: and as for him that wanteth understanding, she saith to him,

[17]Stolen waters are sweet, and bread eaten in secret is pleasant.

[18]But he knoweth not that the dead are there; and that her guests are in the depths of hell.

Wisdom Key

Resist the foolishness of carnal temptations and allow the fear of the Lord and His divine wisdom to lead you in all your ways.

Today's Prayer

Satan often disguises his lies by distorting godly wisdom. Father, help me not to fall prey to these twists in Your truth. Help me to hear Your call of wisdom and turn a deaf ear to the cries of imposters. I will learn to love Your reproofs and rebukes as You take me from the demise of ignorance into the life of understanding.

Q & A with Bishop George Bloomer

When the Spirit of God yanks you from your place of comfort,
how do you fulfill the call of God without acquiescing to the fear
that accompanies it?

Anything that has to do with God is going to produce a
level of fear. Whether this fear is in being petrified, respect, or reverence toward God, when God steps into the
room, the atmosphere is reduced to some level of fear.
When God moves you from your comfort zone to an uncomfortable place, He's developing and building character
in you. He's preparing you to be transported to another
dimension, to be taken to another level. The only thing
you can do is rest in Him and relax in Him. Put your feet
up, enjoy the ride, and enjoy the outcome. He's always taking us to a better place. When God is moving us, there is
nothing that we can do except move with Him, because if
we don't move with God, we're going to be in trouble. This
is because He causes everything around us to change and
to dry up before He moves us. It's the dry places that make
us uncomfortable. So rest and relax in Him.

Today's Positive Achievement

_____

_____

_____

_____

_____

_____

_____

_____

_____

_____

_____

_____

_____

_____

_____

_____

_____

_____

_____

Proverbs 10

¹The proverbs of Solomon. A wise son maketh a glad father: but a foolish son is the heaviness of his mother.

²Treasures of wickedness profit nothing: but righteousness delivereth from death.

³The Lord will not suffer the soul of the righteous to famish: but he casteth away the substance of the wicked.

⁴He becometh poor that dealeth with a slack hand: but the hand of the diligent maketh rich.

⁵He that gathereth in summer is a wise son: but he that sleepeth in harvest is a son that causeth shame.

⁶Blessings are upon the head of the just: but violence covereth the mouth of the wicked.

⁷The memory of the just is blessed: but the name of the wicked shall rot.

⁸The wise in heart will receive commandments: but a prating fool shall fall.

⁹He that walketh uprightly walketh surely: but he that perverteth his ways shall be known.

¹⁰He that winketh with the eye causeth sorrow: but a prating fool shall fall.

¹¹The mouth of a righteous man is a well of life: but violence covereth the mouth of the wicked.

¹²Hatred stirreth up strifes: but love covereth all sins.

¹³In the lips of him that hath understanding wisdom is found: but a rod is for the back of him that is void of understanding.

¹⁴Wise men lay up knowledge: but the mouth of the foolish is near destruction.

¹⁵The rich man's wealth is his strong city: the destruction of the poor is their poverty.

¹⁶The labour of the righteous tendeth to life: the fruit of the wicked to sin.

¹⁷He is in the way of life that keepeth instruction: but he that refuseth reproof erreth.

¹⁸He that hideth hatred with lying lips, and he that uttereth a slander, is a fool.

¹⁹In the multitude of words there wanteth not sin: but he that refraineth his lips is wise.

²⁰The tongue of the just is as choice silver: the heart of the wicked is little worth.

²¹The lips of the righteous feed many: but fools die for want of wisdom.

²²The blessing of the Lord, it maketh rich, and he addeth no sorrow with it.

²³It is as sport to a fool to do mischief: but a man of understanding hath wisdom.

²⁴The fear of the wicked, it shall come upon him: but the desire of the righteous shall be granted.

²⁵As the whirlwind passeth, so is the wicked no more: but the righteous is an everlasting foundation.

²⁶As vinegar to the teeth, and as smoke to the eyes, so is the sluggard to them that send him.

²⁷The fear of the Lord prolongeth days: but the years of the wicked shall be shortened.

²⁸The hope of the righteous shall be gladness: but the expectation of the wicked shall perish.

²⁹The way of the Lord is strength to the upright: but destruction shall be to the workers of iniquity.

³⁰The righteous shall never be removed: but the wicked shall not inhabit the earth.

³¹The mouth of the just bringeth forth wisdom: but the froward tongue shall be cut out.

³²The lips of the righteous know what is acceptable: but the mouth of the wicked speaketh frowardness.

Wisdom Key

One who respects his parents is rich in wisdom and reveals a life
that shows forth great wealth.

Today's Prayer

Lord, I pray that I am able to make You proud with the work of
my hands and the fruit of my lips. Please, teach me to be wise in
all that I say and do. Give me the strength to work hard and the
discretion to save for the future. Help me to be a good steward
over what You have blessed me with, and help me to speak life and
truth into the lives You are allowing me to touch.

Q & A with Bishop George Bloomer

How do parents get out of the home an adult child who can't keep a job and is obviously not capable of taking care of himself or herself for any length of time without returning home over and over again?

In Deuteronomy 32:11–12, this story is told about the Lord and His chosen people, Israel:

As an eagle stirreth up her nest, fluttereth over her young, spreadeth abroad her wings, taketh them, beareth them on her wings: so the LORD alone did lead him, and there was no strange god with him.

To everything there is a time and season. And there is ultimately time for a grown person to get out from under the covering of mom and dad. You simply need to stir the nest of this child. Shut the doors. Do not allow him to continually come back. Force him to grow up. That's wisdom. The eagle places thorns in the nest before she lays eggs and covers the thorns with leaves. After the young are hatched, she teaches them to fly. She teaches them to hunt and how to exist by themselves. After that she kicks up the leaves, exposing the thorns, which makes it impossible for them to return to a comfortable environment, because now they have to become effective in offering back something to society. She then leaves and trusts that they will incorporate her teachings in order to exist in the world without her. You are your children's greatest enemy by continuing to allow them to exist in a comfortable environment without forcing them to utilize the skills that you've taught them to coexist without you. You've become the cushion. When you become the thorn, the children will grow up.

Today's Positive Achievement

_____

_____

_____

_____

_____

_____

_____

_____

_____

_____

_____

_____

_____

_____

_____

_____

_____

_____

_____

Day Eleven

Proverbs 11

[1] A false balance is abomination to the LORD: but a just weight is his delight.
[2] When pride cometh, then cometh shame: but with the lowly is wisdom.
[3] The integrity of the upright shall guide them: but the perverseness of transgressors shall destroy them.
[4] Riches profit not in the day of wrath: but righteousness delivereth from death.
[5] The righteousness of the perfect shall direct his way: but the wicked shall fall by his own wickedness.
[6] The righteousness of the upright shall deliver them: but transgressors shall be taken in their own naughtiness.
[7] When a wicked man dieth, his expectation shall perish: and the hope of unjust men perisheth.
[8] The righteous is delivered out of trouble, and the wicked cometh in his stead.
[9] An hypocrite with his mouth destroyeth his neighbour: but through knowledge shall the just be delivered.
[10] When it goeth well with the righteous, the city rejoiceth: and when the wicked perish, there is shouting.
[11] By the blessing of the upright the city is exalted: but it is overthrown by the mouth of the wicked.
[12] He that is void of wisdom despiseth his neighbour: but a man of understanding holdeth his peace.
[13] A talebearer revealeth secrets: but he that is of a faithful spirit concealeth the matter.
[14] Where no counsel is, the people fall: but in the multitude of counsellors there is safety.
[15] He that is surety for a stranger shall smart for it: and he that hateth suretiship is sure.
[16] A gracious woman retaineth honour: and strong men retain riches.
[17] The merciful man doeth good to his own soul: but he that is cruel troubleth his own flesh.
[18] The wicked worketh a deceitful work: but to him that soweth righteousness shall be a sure reward.
[19] As righteousness tendeth to life: so he that pursueth evil pursueth it to his own death.
[20] They that are of a froward heart are abomination to the LORD: but such as are upright in their way are his delight.
[21] Though hand join in hand, the wicked shall not be unpunished: but the seed of the righteous shall be delivered.
[22] As a jewel of gold in a swine's snout, so is a fair woman which is without discretion.
[23] The desire of the righteous is only good: but the expectation of the wicked is wrath.
[24] There is that scattereth, and yet increaseth; and there is that withholdeth more than is meet, but it tendeth to poverty.
[25] The liberal soul shall be made fat: and he that watereth shall be watered also himself.
[26] He that withholdeth corn, the people shall curse him: but blessing shall be upon the head of him that selleth it.
[27] He that diligently seeketh good procureth favour: but he that seeketh mischief, it shall come unto him.
[28] He that trusteth in his riches shall fall; but the righteous shall flourish as a branch.
[29] He that troubleth his own house shall inherit the wind: and the fool shall be servant to the wise of heart.
[30] The fruit of the righteous is a tree of life; and he that winneth souls is wise.
[31] Behold, the righteous shall be recompensed in the earth: much more the wicked and the sinner.

Wisdom Key

Pride reveals a foolish heart, but the righteous and pure in heart
retain their wealth.

Today's Prayer

I need to guard my heart at all times and protect my spirit from
being tainted by the corruption that surrounds me. Father, wash
me clean from all impurity. Help me to prudently display Your
grace and mercy to a world in need of the light that only You can
provide. I want to delight You, Father. I want to be wise and gener-
ous. Teach me to have the character and integrity that I need to be
successful and to bring honor to Your name.

Q & A with Bishop George Bloomer

When you've grown in the wisdom of God but are surrounded by those who've stunted their own growth, how do you continue to walk in the wisdom and instruction of God?

You can't. Filthy communication corrupts good manners. Iron sharpens iron. If you're going to develop yourself, you have to cut the cord between negative, unequally yoked, going-nowhere people. You may have some sort of allegiance or attachment to them for several reasons. Perhaps they introduced you to the Lord, or you've been friends for years and years, but one must know when friendship has moved from friendship to leaching, or from friendship to draining. It takes the wisdom of God to make that direct timing, to make that move, to get away from them, but you must leave them.

Today's Positive Achievement

_____
_____
_____
_____
_____
_____
_____
_____
_____
_____
_____
_____
_____
_____
_____
_____
_____
_____
_____
_____
_____
_____
_____
_____

Day Twelve

Proverbs 12

¹Whoso loveth instruction loveth knowledge: but he that hateth reproof is brutish.

²A good man obtaineth favour of the LORD: but a man of wicked devices will he condemn.

³A man shall not be established by wickedness: but the root of the righteous shall not be moved.

⁴A virtuous woman is a crown to her husband: but she that maketh ashamed is as rottenness in his bones.

⁵The thoughts of the righteous are right: but the counsels of the wicked are deceit.

⁶The words of the wicked are to lie in wait for blood: but the mouth of the upright shall deliver them.

⁷The wicked are overthrown, and are not: but the house of the righteous shall stand.

⁸A man shall be commended according to his wisdom: but he that is of a perverse heart shall be despised.

⁹He that is despised, and hath a servant, is better than he that honoureth himself, and lacketh bread.

¹⁰A righteous man regardeth the life of his beast: but the tender mercies of the wicked are cruel.

¹¹He that tilleth his land shall be satisfied with bread: but he that followeth vain persons is void of understanding.

¹²The wicked desireth the net of evil men: but the root of the righteous yieldeth fruit.

¹³The wicked is snared by the transgression of his lips: but the just shall come out of trouble.

¹⁴A man shall be satisfied with good by the fruit of his mouth: and the recompence of a man's hands shall be rendered unto him.

¹⁵The way of a fool is right in his own eyes: but he that hearkeneth unto counsel is wise.

¹⁶A fool's wrath is presently known: but a prudent man covereth shame.

¹⁷He that speaketh truth sheweth forth righteousness: but a false witness deceit.

¹⁸There is that speaketh like the piercings of a sword: but the tongue of the wise is health.

¹⁹The lip of truth shall be established for ever: but a lying tongue is but for a moment.

²⁰Deceit is in the heart of them that imagine evil: but to the counsellors of peace is joy.

²¹There shall no evil happen to the just: but the wicked shall be filled with mischief.

²²Lying lips are abomination to the LORD: but they that deal truly are his delight.

²³A prudent man concealeth knowledge: but the heart of fools proclaimeth foolishness.

²⁴The hand of the diligent shall bear rule: but the slothful shall be under tribute.

²⁵Heaviness in the heart of man maketh it stoop: but a good word maketh it glad.

²⁶The righteous is more excellent than his neighbour: but the way of the wicked seduceth them.

²⁷The slothful man roasteth not that which he took in hunting: but the substance of a diligent man is precious.

²⁸In the way of righteousness is life: and in the pathway thereof there is no death.

Wisdom Key

To have great regard and respect for others is to secure honor and regard for one's self.

Today's Prayer

Father God, help me to love and respect all people. I pray that I will always treat myself and others with dignity and honor. Help me to exemplify You in my personal dealings and my social interactions.

Q & A with Bishop George Bloomer

Today, does it matter if the husband stays home to raise the kids
while the wife goes out to work?

No. It doesn't matter. What works for you, works for you.

Today's Positive Achievement

_____

_____

_____

_____

_____

_____

_____

_____

_____

_____

_____

_____

_____

_____

_____

_____

_____

_____

_____

_____

_____

_____

_____

Day Thirteen

Proverbs 13

¹A wise son heareth his father's instruction: but a scorner heareth not rebuke.

²A man shall eat good by the fruit of his mouth: but the soul of the transgressors shall eat violence.

³He that keepeth his mouth keepeth his life: but he that openeth wide his lips shall have destruction.

⁴The soul of the sluggard desireth, and hath nothing: but the soul of the diligent shall be made fat.

⁵A righteous man hateth lying: but a wicked man is loathsome, and cometh to shame.

⁶Righteousness keepeth him that is upright in the way: but wickedness overthroweth the sinner.

⁷There is that maketh himself rich, yet hath nothing: there is that maketh himself poor, yet hath great riches.

⁸The ransom of a man's life are his riches: but the poor heareth not rebuke.

⁹The light of the righteous rejoiceth: but the lamp of the wicked shall be put out.

¹⁰Only by pride cometh contention: but with the well advised is wisdom.

¹¹Wealth gotten by vanity shall be diminished: but he that gathereth by labour shall increase.

¹²Hope deferred maketh the heart sick: but when the desire cometh, it is a tree of life.

¹³Whoso despiseth the word shall be destroyed: but he that feareth the commandment shall be rewarded.

¹⁴The law of the wise is a fountain of life, to depart from the snares of death.

¹⁵Good understanding giveth favour: but the way of transgressors is hard.

¹⁶Every prudent man dealeth with knowledge: but a fool layeth open his folly.

¹⁷A wicked messenger falleth into mischief: but a faithful ambassador is health.

¹⁸Poverty and shame shall be to him that refuseth instruction: but he that regardeth reproof shall be honoured.

¹⁹The desire accomplished is sweet to the soul: but it is abomination to fools to depart from evil.

²⁰He that walketh with wise men shall be wise: but a companion of fools shall be destroyed.

²¹Evil pursueth sinners: but to the righteous good shall be repayed.

²²A good man leaveth an inheritance to his children's children: and the wealth of the sinner is laid up for the just.

²³Much food is in the tillage of the poor: but there is that is destroyed for want of judgment.

²⁴He that spareth his rod hateth his son: but he that loveth him chasteneth him betimes.

²⁵The righteous eateth to the satisfying of his soul: but the belly of the wicked shall want.

Wisdom Key

A wise man in his life covers his home with all diligence, and in death leaves an inheritance for his children's children.

Today's Prayer

I pray, in the name of Jesus, that my supplication for wisdom and understanding reaches the throne of heaven. Open my spiritual ears and eyes. Help me to see and hear all that you are communicating with me. Teach me to be righteous, pure, and upright in everything I say and do. *"As for me and my house, we will serve the Lord"* (Joshua 24:15) is the banner of protection and salvation that I place over myself and my family.

Q & A with Bishop George Bloomer

What are the primary principles to instill in children today who are faced with insurmountable peer pressure to go against everything that they've been taught by their parents?

I don't really know the answer to that. I say this because it seems to me that today no matter how structured a family is or how wholesome and pure it is—where the dad and mom are religious, good, upright, and moral people—that time plus time equals influence. Environment changes character, and communication changes manners. Filthy communication develops desires that go against the rules, principles, and moral laws that were set in the hearts of our children. So, the answer to the question is to teach at a young age the things that are right. Then, try—in as much as you can—to interview your children as friends while maintaining the parental role. Furthermore, be a host for the other kids in the community to come to your house, instead of your children always going to other houses. I remember when my kids were growing up, I was a great host, so everybody wanted to come to our house. This way, you control what goes on in that environment, and the other kids are asking your children, "Can I come over to your house?" versus your children asking you, "Mom, can I go over to their house?"

Today's Positive Achievement

_____

_____

_____

_____

_____

_____

_____

_____

_____

_____

_____

_____

_____

_____

_____

_____

_____

_____

_____

_____

_____

_____

Day Fourteen

Proverbs 14

¹Every wise woman buildeth her house: but the foolish plucketh it down with her hands.

²He that walketh in his uprightness feareth the LORD: but he that is perverse in his ways despiseth him.

³In the mouth of the foolish is a rod of pride: but the lips of the wise shall preserve them.

⁴Where no oxen are, the crib is clean: but much increase is by the strength of the ox.

⁵A faithful witness will not lie: but a false witness will utter lies.

⁶A scorner seeketh wisdom, and findeth it not: but knowledge is easy unto him that understandeth.

⁷Go from the presence of a foolish man, when thou perceivest not in him the lips of knowledge.

⁸The wisdom of the prudent is to understand his way: but the folly of fools is deceit.

⁹Fools make a mock at sin: but among the righteous there is favour.

¹⁰The heart knoweth his own bitterness; and a stranger doth not intermeddle with his joy.

¹¹The house of the wicked shall be overthrown: but the tabernacle of the upright shall flourish.

¹²There is a way which seemeth right unto a man, but the end thereof are the ways of death.

¹³Even in laughter the heart is sorrowful; and the end of that mirth is heaviness.

¹⁴The backslider in heart shall be filled with his own ways: and a good man shall be satisfied from himself.

¹⁵The simple believeth every word: but the prudent man looketh well to his going.

¹⁶A wise man feareth, and departeth from evil: but the fool rageth, and is confident.

¹⁷He that is soon angry dealeth foolishly: and a man of wicked devices is hated.

¹⁸The simple inherit folly: but the prudent are crowned with knowledge.

¹⁹The evil bow before the good; and the wicked at the gates of the righteous.

²⁰The poor is hated even of his own neighbour: but the rich hath many friends.

²¹He that despiseth his neighbour sinneth: but he that hath mercy on the poor, happy is he.

²²Do they not err that devise evil? but mercy and truth shall be to them that devise good.

²³In all labour there is profit: but the talk of the lips tendeth only to penury.

²⁴The crown of the wise is their riches: but the foolishness of fools is folly.

²⁵A true witness delivereth souls: but a deceitful witness speaketh lies.

²⁶In the fear of the LORD is strong confidence: and his children shall have a place of refuge.

²⁷The fear of the LORD is a fountain of life, to depart from the snares of death.

²⁸In the multitude of people is the king's honour: but in the want of people is the destruction of the prince.

²⁹He that is slow to wrath is of great understanding: but he that is hasty of spirit exalteth folly.

³⁰A sound heart is the life of the flesh: but envy the rottenness of the bones.

³¹He that oppresseth the poor reproacheth his Maker: but he that honoureth him hath mercy on the poor.

³²The wicked is driven away in his wickedness: but the righteous hath hope in his death.

³³Wisdom resteth in the heart of him that hath understanding: but that which is in the midst of fools is made known.

³⁴Righteousness exalteth a nation: but sin is a reproach to any people.

³⁵The king's favour is toward a wise servant: but his wrath is against him that causeth shame.

Wisdom Key

A wise woman realizes the value of her spoken word and a wicked woman wallows in her own deceit.

Today's Prayer

Help me to open up the pains and hurts I have from the past to You, Lord, so that I can grow into the wise person You designed me to be. I was fearfully and wonderfully made by You, and You knew me before the creation of the world. You know each scar that has been left on my heart. So, today, I lift myself—body, soul, and spirit—up to You, Father, and I ask you to heal, renew, cleanse, and fortify every inch of me. Give me the courage to walk in the freedom and restoration that You provide daily.

Q & A with Bishop George Bloomer

How can the love of God shine through a person who has known
nothing but bitterness throughout his or her entire life?

That's very, very easy. By the love of God being revealed
to him or her. The love of God is revealed to us in many
ways: through laughter, odors—the smell of flowers, fresh
cut grass, a homemade baked pie, fresh baked cookies—
through touching, smelling, hearing and tasting. You gain
an appreciation for life by noticing the small things, and
once a great appreciation for life comes, you begin to gather a greater appreciation for the Creator of life. Just look
around you. God is everywhere and His love and appreciation for life is everywhere.

Today's Positive Achievement

_____

_____

_____

_____

_____

_____

_____

_____

_____

_____

_____

_____

_____

_____

_____

_____

_____

_____

_____

_____

_____

Day Fifteen

Proverbs 15

¹A soft answer turneth away wrath: but grievous words stir up anger. ²The tongue of the wise useth knowledge aright: but the mouth of fools poureth out foolishness. ³The eyes of the LORD are in every place, beholding the evil and the good. ⁴A wholesome tongue is a tree of life: but perverseness therein is a breach in the spirit. ⁵A fool despiseth his father's instruction: but he that regardeth reproof is prudent. ⁶In the house of the righteous is much treasure: but in the revenues of the wicked is trouble. ⁷The lips of the wise disperse knowledge: but the heart of the foolish doeth not so. ⁸The sacrifice of the wicked is an abomination to the LORD: but the prayer of the upright is his delight. ⁹The way of the wicked is an abomination unto the LORD: but he loveth him that followeth after righteousness. ¹⁰Correction is grievous unto him that forsaketh the way: and he that hateth reproof shall die. ¹¹Hell and destruction are before the LORD: how much more then the hearts of the children of men? ¹²A scorner loveth not one that reproveth him: neither will he go unto the wise. ¹³A merry heart maketh a cheerful countenance: but by sorrow of the heart the spirit is broken. ¹⁴The heart of him that hath understanding seeketh knowledge: but the mouth of fools feedeth on foolishness. ¹⁵All the days of the afflicted are evil: but he that is of a merry heart hath a continual feast. ¹⁶Better is little with the fear of the LORD than great treasure and trouble therewith. ¹⁷Better is a dinner of herbs where love is, than a stalled ox and hatred therewith. ¹⁸A wrathful man stirreth up strife: but he that is slow to anger appeaseth strife. ¹⁹The way of the slothful man is as an hedge of thorns: but the way of the righteous is made plain. ²⁰A wise son maketh a glad father: but a foolish man despiseth his mother. ²¹Folly is joy to him that is destitute of wisdom: but a man of understanding walketh uprightly. ²²Without counsel purposes are disappointed: but in the multitude of counsellors they are established. ²³A man hath joy by the answer of his mouth: and a word spoken in due season, how good is it! ²⁴The way of life is above to the wise, that he may depart from hell beneath. ²⁵The LORD will destroy the house of the proud: but he will establish the border of the widow. ²⁶The thoughts of the wicked are an abomination to the LORD: but the words of the pure are pleasant words. ²⁷He that is greedy of gain troubleth his own house; but he that hateth gifts shall live. ²⁸The heart of the righteous studieth to answer: but the mouth of the wicked poureth out evil things. ²⁹The LORD is far from the wicked: but he heareth the prayer of the righteous. ³⁰The light of the eyes rejoiceth the heart: and a good report maketh the bones fat. ³¹The ear that heareth the reproof of life abideth among the wise. ³²He that refuseth instruction despiseth his own soul: but he that heareth reproof getteth understanding. ³³The fear of the LORD is the instruction of wisdom; and before honour is humility.

Wisdom Key

Anger is the fuel that ignites the fire of disputes and pain, but a peaceful response smothers the flames.

Today's Prayer

I speak peace into my life. Everywhere I go, every place my feet tread, serenity will abide. The presence of God drives out all chaos, and the wisdom of God drives out all confusion. My mind and my life have been consecrated unto God; therefore, turmoil, disorder, and mayhem have no authority over me.

Q & A with Bishop George Bloomer

How can a believer allow patience to have her perfect work when chaos is breaking out all around?

Notice the Scripture tells us to *"let patience have her perfect work"* in you. (See James 1:4.) The "how-can" is a revelation to "how can you not." In the midst of struggles, strife and problems, one is always seeking wisdom and knowledge that leads to a place called peace. So stop focusing so much on the negativity and get quiet. In the quietness, the peace of God that passes all human understanding will overtake you, your mind, your body, and your soul.

Today's Positive Achievements

_____

_____

_____

_____

_____

_____

_____

_____

_____

_____

_____

_____

_____

_____

_____

_____

_____

_____

_____

_____

_____

Proverbs 16

¹The preparations of the heart in man, and the answer of the tongue, is from the Lord.

²All the ways of a man are clean in his own eyes; but the Lord weigheth the spirits.

³Commit thy works unto the Lord, and thy thoughts shall be established.

⁴The Lord hath made all things for himself: yea, even the wicked for the day of evil.

⁵Every one that is proud in heart is an abomination to the Lord: though hand join in hand, he shall not be unpunished.

⁶By mercy and truth iniquity is purged: and by the fear of the Lord men depart from evil.

⁷When a man's ways please the Lord, he maketh even his enemies to be at peace with him.

⁸Better is a little with righteousness than great revenues without right.

⁹A man's heart deviseth his way: but the Lord directeth his steps.

¹⁰A divine sentence is in the lips of the king: his mouth transgresseth not in judgment.

¹¹A just weight and balance are the Lord's: all the weights of the bag are his work.

¹²It is an abomination to kings to commit wickedness: for the throne is established by righteousness.

¹³Righteous lips are the delight of kings; and they love him that speaketh right.

¹⁴The wrath of a king is as messengers of death: but a wise man will pacify it.

¹⁵In the light of the king's countenance is life; and his favour is as a cloud of the latter rain.

¹⁶How much better is it to get wisdom than gold! and to get understanding rather to be chosen than silver!

¹⁷The highway of the upright is to depart from evil: he that keepeth his way preserveth his soul.

¹⁸Pride goeth before destruction, and an haughty spirit before a fall.

¹⁹Better it is to be of an humble spirit with the lowly, than to divide the spoil with the proud.

²⁰He that handleth a matter wisely shall find good: and whoso trusteth in the Lord, happy is he.

²¹The wise in heart shall be called prudent: and the sweetness of the lips increaseth learning.

²²Understanding is a wellspring of life unto him that hath it: but the instruction of fools is folly.

²³The heart of the wise teacheth his mouth, and addeth learning to his lips.

²⁴Pleasant words are as an honeycomb, sweet to the soul, and health to the bones.

²⁵There is a way that seemeth right unto a man, but the end thereof are the ways of death.

²⁶He that laboureth laboureth for himself; for his mouth craveth it of him.

²⁷An ungodly man diggeth up evil: and in his lips there is as a burning fire.

²⁸A froward man soweth strife: and a whisperer separateth chief friends.

²⁹A violent man enticeth his neighbour, and leadeth him into the way that is not good.

³⁰He shutteth his eyes to devise froward things: moving his lips he bringeth evil to pass.

³¹The hoary head is a crown of glory, if it be found in the way of righteousness.

³²He that is slow to anger is better than the mighty; and he that ruleth his spirit than he that taketh a city.

³³The lot is cast into the lap; but the whole disposing thereof is of the Lord.

Wisdom Key

You can predict the severity of a man's fall tomorrow by the height of his arrogance and pride today.

Today's Prayer

Father, take all traces of arrogance, superiority, and haughtiness out of my heart. Teach me humility and meekness as I realize that this life isn't about me, but instead about You and Your eternal plan.

Q & A with Bishop George Bloomer

In today's society when everyone is looking out for number one, how do you guard your heart against these attitudes of greed, pride, arrogance, and callousness?

The one sure way is by keeping your mind focused on Christ. Isaiah 26:3 says, *"Thou wilt keep him in perfect peace, whose mind is stayed on thee: because he trusteth in thee."* Follow your conscience.

Today's Positive Achievement

_____

_____

_____

_____

_____

_____

_____

_____

_____

_____

_____

_____

_____

_____

_____

_____

_____

_____

_____

_____

_____

Day Seventeen

Proverbs 17

¹Better is a dry morsel, and quietness therewith, than an house full of sacrifices with strife.

²A wise servant shall have rule over a son that causeth shame, and shall have part of the inheritance among the brethren.

³The fining pot is for silver, and the furnace for gold: but the LORD trieth the hearts.

⁴A wicked doer giveth heed to false lips; and a liar giveth ear to a naughty tongue.

⁵Whoso mocketh the poor reproacheth his Maker: and he that is glad at calamities shall not be unpunished.

⁶Children's children are the crown of old men; and the glory of children are their fathers.

⁷Excellent speech becometh not a fool: much less do lying lips a prince.

⁸A gift is as a precious stone in the eyes of him that hath it: whithersoever it turneth, it prospereth.

⁹He that covereth a transgression seeketh love; but he that repeateth a matter separateth very friends.

¹⁰A reproof entereth more into a wise man than an hundred stripes into a fool.

¹¹An evil man seeketh only rebellion: therefore a cruel messenger shall be sent against him.

¹²Let a bear robbed of her whelps meet a man, rather than a fool in his folly.

¹³Whoso rewardeth evil for good, evil shall not depart from his house.

¹⁴The beginning of strife is as when one letteth out water: therefore leave off contention, before it be meddled with.

¹⁵He that justifieth the wicked, and he that condemneth the just, even they both are abomination to the LORD.

¹⁶Wherefore is there a price in the hand of a fool to get wisdom, seeing he hath no heart to it?

¹⁷A friend loveth at all times, and a brother is born for adversity.

¹⁸A man void of understanding striketh hands, and becometh surety in the presence of his friend.

¹⁹He loveth transgression that loveth strife: and he that exalteth his gate seeketh destruction.

²⁰He that hath a froward heart findeth no good: and he that hath a perverse tongue falleth into mischief.

²¹He that begetteth a fool doeth it to his sorrow: and the father of a fool hath no joy.

²²A merry heart doeth good like a medicine: but a broken spirit drieth the bones.

²³A wicked man taketh a gift out of the bosom to pervert the ways of judgment.

²⁴Wisdom is before him that hath understanding; but the eyes of a fool are in the ends of the earth.

²⁵A foolish son is a grief to his father, and bitterness to her that bare him.

²⁶Also to punish the just is not good, nor to strike princes for equity.

²⁷He that hath knowledge spareth his words: and a man of understanding is of an excellent spirit.

²⁸Even a fool, when he holdeth his peace, is counted wise: and he that shutteth his lips is esteemed a man of understanding.

Wisdom Key

Sleep rejuvenates the wise and makes him creative for that day, but fools live in dreamland.

Today's Prayer

Father, I pray I waste none of the time You have given me on this earth chasing after fruitless, childish dreams. Help me to set my heart on what's achievable and to relentlessly follow each God-idea You give me. I pray You place the spirit of creativity on my life. Help me to be about my Father's business as I successfully orchestrate and implement the purpose You have predestined for me.

Q & A with Bishop George Bloomer

If you are dating someone who is constantly pursuing a new dream, without ever taking the initiative to bring any of the dreams to fruition, should you continue to support this person's visions or walk away and focus on the dreams that you have for yourself?

First of all, you should never stop focusing on your own dreams and aspirations, whether you're assisting someone else's or not. Never become so engulfed by another person's dreams that you eventually give up on your own. And when dealing with a dreamer who's not taking the initiative to fulfill his/her dreams, you should simply be honest with this person. To continue supporting dead dreams only hurts the individual and feeds your lack of fulfillment.

Today's Positive Achievement

Day Eighteen

Proverbs 18

¹Through desire a man, having separated himself, seeketh and intermeddleth with all wisdom.

²A fool hath no delight in understanding, but that his heart may discover itself.

³When the wicked cometh, then cometh also contempt, and with ignominy reproach.

⁴The words of a man's mouth are as deep waters, and the wellspring of wisdom as a flowing brook.

⁵It is not good to accept the person of the wicked, to overthrow the righteous in judgment.

⁶A fool's lips enter into contention, and his mouth calleth for strokes.

⁷A fool's mouth is his destruction, and his lips are the snare of his soul.

⁸The words of a talebearer are as wounds, and they go down into the innermost parts of the belly.

⁹He also that is slothful in his work is brother to him that is a great waster.

¹⁰The name of the Lord is a strong tower: the righteous runneth into it, and is safe.

¹¹The rich man's wealth is his strong city, and as an high wall in his own conceit.

¹²Before destruction the heart of man is haughty, and before honour is humility.

¹³He that answereth a matter before he heareth it, it is folly and shame unto him.

¹⁴The spirit of a man will sustain his infirmity; but a wounded spirit who can bear?

¹⁵The heart of the prudent getteth knowledge; and the ear of the wise seeketh knowledge.

¹⁶A man's gift maketh room for him, and bringeth him before great men.

¹⁷He that is first in his own cause seemeth just; but his neighbour cometh and searcheth him.

¹⁸The lot causeth contentions to cease, and parteth between the mighty.

¹⁹A brother offended is harder to be won than a strong city: and their contentions are like the bars of a castle.

²⁰A man's belly shall be satisfied with the fruit of his mouth; and with the increase of his lips shall he be filled.

²¹Death and life are in the power of the tongue: and they that love it shall eat the fruit thereof.

²²Whoso findeth a wife findeth a good thing, and obtaineth favour of the Lord.

²³The poor useth intreaties; but the rich answereth roughly.

²⁴A man that hath friends must shew himself friendly: and there is a friend that sticketh closer than a brother.

Wisdom Key

Passing the buck and getting away with it may make you a cunning person, but in the end, your cunningness robs you of true relationships.

Today's Prayer

To have a friend, one must be a friend. Lord, teach me to be a friend and to put others before myself. Help me to see the good in the people around me instead of judging others so that I feel better about myself. Open my heart, Father, and help me to love unconditionally so that I can truly represent You.

Q & A with Bishop George Bloomer

When the fear of divorce forces you to live a marriage that's based on lies, how do you ever gain the courage to face the truth?

When you live in a situation that's based on lies, "lie" becomes your truth, and truth becomes impossible. The only way to free yourself from that is to embrace God, ask Him for His wisdom and His timing. While I am not advocating divorce, I am admonishing you to take the necessary steps toward facing truth. Make your move, and the Lord will take care of you. To stay in the same predicament further places you in the quagmire that deeply entrenches you into the lie and makes it impossible for you to live in reality.

Today's Positive Achievement

_____

_____

_____

_____

_____

_____

_____

_____

_____

_____

_____

_____

_____

_____

_____

_____

_____

_____

_____

_____

_____

_____

_____

_____

Proverbs 19

¹Better is the poor that walketh in his integrity, than he that is perverse in his lips, and is a fool.

²Also, that the soul be without knowledge, it is not good; and he that hasteth with his feet sinneth.

³The foolishness of man perverteth his way: and his heart fretteth against the LORD.

⁴Wealth maketh many friends; but the poor is separated from his neighbour.

⁵A false witness shall not be unpunished, and he that speaketh lies shall not escape.

⁶Many will intreat the favour of the prince: and every man is a friend to him that giveth gifts.

⁷All the brethren of the poor do hate him: how much more do his friends go far from him? he pursueth them with words, yet they are wanting to him.

⁸He that getteth wisdom loveth his own soul: he that keepeth understanding shall find good.

⁹A false witness shall not be unpunished, and he that speaketh lies shall perish.

¹⁰Delight is not seemly for a fool; much less for a servant to have rule over princes.

¹¹The discretion of a man deferreth his anger; and it is his glory to pass over a transgression.

¹²The king's wrath is as the roaring of a lion; but his favour is as dew upon the grass.

¹³A foolish son is the calamity of his father: and the contentions of a wife are a continual dropping.

¹⁴House and riches are the inheritance of fathers: and a prudent wife is from the LORD.

¹⁵Slothfulness casteth into a deep sleep; and an idle soul shall suffer hunger.

¹⁶He that keepeth the commandment keepeth his own soul; but he that despiseth his ways shall die.

¹⁷He that hath pity upon the poor lendeth unto the LORD; and that which he hath given will he pay him again.

¹⁸Chasten thy son while there is hope, and let not thy soul spare for his crying.

¹⁹A man of great wrath shall suffer punishment: for if thou deliver him, yet thou must do it again.

²⁰Hear counsel, and receive instruction, that thou mayest be wise in thy latter end.

²¹There are many devices in a man's heart; nevertheless the counsel of the LORD, that shall stand.

²²The desire of a man is his kindness: and a poor man is better than a liar.

²³The fear of the LORD tendeth to life: and he that hath it shall abide satisfied; he shall not be visited with evil.

²⁴A slothful man hideth his hand in his bosom, and will not so much as bring it to his mouth again.

²⁵Smite a scorner, and the simple will beware: and reprove one that hath understanding, and he will understand knowledge.

²⁶He that wasteth his father, and chaseth away his mother, is a son that causeth shame, and bringeth reproach.

²⁷Cease, my son, to hear the instruction that causeth to err from the words of knowledge.

²⁸An ungodly witness scorneth judgment: and the mouth of the wicked devoureth iniquity.

²⁹Judgments are prepared for scorners, and stripes for the back of fools.

Wisdom Key

It's easier to follow the deceitfulness of the crowd than follow the morals of your heart.

Today's Prayer

Fear of the Lord leads to life, and it is the beginning of wisdom. As Your child, help my fear and reverence of You to lead me to do what is right in all situations. Establish integrity within my heart and mind so I will do what's right even when no one else is around.

Q & A with Bishop George Bloomer

How do parents teach their children to have reverential fear of authority while still encouraging them to challenge the status quo and think outside the box?

Today we live in a society where authority is abused so often that parents must use wisdom and caution when teaching reverence. Be careful to decisively differentiate between authority and abuse so that your children will not fear challenging abuse of authority as opposed to respecting proper authority. Teach your children to take instructions, but at the same time not to be afraid of challenging the boundaries of their own creative minds.

Today's Positive Achievement

_____

_____

_____

_____

_____

_____

_____

_____

_____

_____

_____

_____

_____

_____

_____

_____

_____

_____

_____

_____

_____

Proverbs 20

¹Wine is a mocker, strong drink is raging: and whosoever is deceived thereby is not wise.

²The fear of a king is as the roaring of a lion: whoso provoketh him to anger sinneth against his own soul.

³It is an honour for a man to cease from strife: but every fool will be meddling.

⁴The sluggard will not plow by reason of the cold; therefore shall he beg in harvest, and have nothing.

⁵Counsel in the heart of man is like deep water; but a man of understanding will draw it out.

⁶Most men will proclaim every one his own goodness: but a faithful man who can find?

⁷The just man walketh in his integrity: his children are blessed after him.

⁸A king that sitteth in the throne of judgment scattereth away all evil with his eyes.

⁹Who can say, I have made my heart clean, I am pure from my sin?

¹⁰Divers weights, and divers measures, both of them are alike abomination to the LORD.

¹¹Even a child is known by his doings, whether his work be pure, and whether it be right.

¹²The hearing ear, and the seeing eye, the LORD hath made even both of them.

¹³Love not sleep, lest thou come to poverty; open thine eyes, and thou shalt be satisfied with bread.

¹⁴It is naught, it is naught, saith the buyer: but when he is gone his way, then he boasteth.

¹⁵There is gold, and a multitude of rubies: but the lips of knowledge are a precious jewel.

¹⁶Take his garment that is surety for a stranger: and take a pledge of him for a strange woman.

¹⁷Bread of deceit is sweet to a man; but afterwards his mouth shall be filled with gravel.

¹⁸Every purpose is established by counsel: and with good advice make war.

¹⁹He that goeth about as a talebearer revealeth secrets: therefore meddle not with him that flattereth with his lips.

²⁰Whoso curseth his father or his mother, his lamp shall be put out in obscure darkness.

²¹An inheritance may be gotten hastily at the beginning; but the end thereof shall not be blessed.

²²Say not thou, I will recompense evil; but wait on the LORD, and he shall save thee.

²³Divers weights are an abomination unto the LORD; and a false balance is not good.

²⁴Man's goings are of the LORD; how can a man then understand his own way?

²⁵It is a snare to the man who devoureth that which is holy, and after vows to make enquiry.

²⁶A wise king scattereth the wicked, and bringeth the wheel over them.

²⁷The spirit of man is the candle of the LORD, searching all the inward parts of the belly.

²⁸Mercy and truth preserve the king: and his throne is upholden by mercy.

²⁹The glory of young men is their strength: and the beauty of old men is the grey head.

³⁰The blueness of a wound cleanseth away evil: so do stripes the inward parts of the belly.

Wisdom Key

The best way to judge good character is the ability to chastise one's self.

Today's Prayer

Father, help me to walk in a way that will bring blessings on my life and on the lives of my children and my children's children. Help me to acknowledge when I have strayed from Your truth or Your will so I can pull myself back on course, and help me to admit when I have missed the mark so I can humbly apologize to the people You have placed in my life. Never allow me to get so comfortable in my walk with You that I forget to inspect my life daily for evidence of Your presence in me.

Q & A with Bishop George Bloomer

What is the difference between correcting myself and beating myself up? How do I honestly rebuke myself without crossing the line and abusing myself?

While this is a very good question, most people do not rebuke themselves. It has to be pointed out to most people that what they have done is wrong. However, for the rare few who do correct themselves, they can use Jesus' example. He said, *"For God sent not his Son into the world to condemn the world; but that the world through him might be saved"* (John 3:17). If Jesus didn't come to condemn you, then neither should you condemn yourself. Acknowledge your wrongdoings, take the necessary steps to correct them, repent, and move on.

Today's Positive Achievement

Day Twenty-One

Proverbs 21

¹The king's heart is in the hand of the LORD, as the rivers of water: he turneth it whithersoever he will.

²Every way of a man is right in his own eyes: but the LORD pondereth the hearts.

³To do justice and judgment is more acceptable to the LORD than sacrifice.

⁴An high look, and a proud heart, and the plowing of the wicked, is sin.

⁵The thoughts of the diligent tend only to plenteousness; but of every one that is hasty only to want.

⁶The getting of treasures by a lying tongue is a vanity tossed to and fro of them that seek death.

⁷The robbery of the wicked shall destroy them; because they refuse to do judgment.

⁸The way of man is froward and strange: but as for the pure, his work is right.

⁹It is better to dwell in a corner of the housetop, than with a brawling woman in a wide house.

¹⁰The soul of the wicked desireth evil: his neighbour findeth no favour in his eyes.

¹¹When the scorner is punished, the simple is made wise: and when the wise is instructed, he receiveth knowledge.

¹²The righteous man wisely considereth the house of the wicked: but God overthroweth the wicked for their wickedness.

¹³Whoso stoppeth his ears at the cry of the poor, he also shall cry himself, but shall not be heard.

¹⁴A gift in secret pacifieth anger: and a reward in the bosom strong wrath.

¹⁵It is joy to the just to do judgment: but destruction shall be to the workers of iniquity.

¹⁶The man that wandereth out of the way of understanding shall remain in the congregation of the dead.

¹⁷He that loveth pleasure shall be a poor man: he that loveth wine and oil shall not be rich.

¹⁸The wicked shall be a ransom for the righteous, and the transgressor for the upright.

¹⁹It is better to dwell in the wilderness, than with a contentious and an angry woman.

²⁰There is treasure to be desired and oil in the dwelling of the wise; but a foolish man spendeth it up.

²¹He that followeth after righteousness and mercy findeth life, righteousness, and honour.

²²A wise man scaleth the city of the mighty, and casteth down the strength of the confidence thereof.

²³Whoso keepeth his mouth and his tongue keepeth his soul from troubles.

²⁴Proud and haughty scorner is his name, who dealeth in proud wrath.

²⁵The desire of the slothful killeth him; for his hands refuse to labour.

²⁶He coveteth greedily all the day long: but the righteous giveth and spareth not.

²⁷The sacrifice of the wicked is abomination: how much more, when he bringeth it with a wicked mind?

²⁸A false witness shall perish: but the man that heareth speaketh constantly.

²⁹A wicked man hardeneth his face: but as for the upright, he directeth his way.

³⁰There is no wisdom nor understanding nor counsel against the LORD.

³¹The horse is prepared against the day of battle: but safety is of the LORD.

Wisdom Key

Personal integrity is feeling bad for doing something that only you know that you've done.

Today's Prayer

Wisdom and integrity must work together; neither can stand without the other. So, Father, I am asking that You give me the wisdom and integrity to do what is pleasing in Your sight always.

Q & A with Bishop George Bloomer

When I was 18 and working my first job, I stole $30 from the cash register. Now that I am older, wiser, and saved, I feel guilty, but the business has closed, and I don't know what to do to make it right. Is this guilt coming from God or is it condemnation that I should let go of?

Both! You do owe the company $30, and your conscience is demanding that you pay. You took an unauthorized loan from your former employer. Give the amount you owe, plus interest, to charity. Repay the debt, and recognize the fact that your desire and attempt to right your wrong is evidence of a sincere heart. God knows the difference between sincerity and deceitfulness, *"for the LORD seeth not as man seeth; for man looketh on the outward appearance, but the LORD looketh on the heart"* (1 Samuel 16:7).

Today's Positive Achievement

_____

_____

_____

_____

_____

_____

_____

_____

_____

_____

_____

_____

_____

_____

_____

_____

_____

_____

_____

_____

_____

_____

Day Twenty-two

Proverbs 22

¹A good name is rather to be chosen than great riches, and loving favour rather than silver and gold.

²The rich and poor meet together: the LORD is the maker of them all.

³A prudent man foreseeth the evil, and hideth himself: but the simple pass on, and are punished.

⁴By humility and the fear of the LORD are riches, and honour, and life.

⁵Thorns and snares are in the way of the froward: he that doth keep his soul shall be far from them.

⁶Train up a child in the way he should go: and when he is old, he will not depart from it.

⁷The rich ruleth over the poor, and the borrower is servant to the lender.

⁸He that soweth iniquity shall reap vanity: and the rod of his anger shall fail.

⁹He that hath a bountiful eye shall be blessed; for he giveth of his bread to the poor.

¹⁰Cast out the scorner, and contention shall go out; yea, strife and reproach shall cease.

¹¹He that loveth pureness of heart, for the grace of his lips the king shall be his friend.

¹²The eyes of the LORD preserve knowledge, and he overthroweth the words of the transgressor.

¹³The slothful man saith, There is a lion without, I shall be slain in the streets.

¹⁴The mouth of strange women is a deep pit: he that is abhorred of the LORD shall fall therein.

¹⁵Foolishness is bound in the heart of a child; but the rod of correction shall drive it far from him.

¹⁶He that oppresseth the poor to increase his riches, and he that giveth to the rich, shall surely come to want.

¹⁷Bow down thine ear, and hear the words of the wise, and apply thine heart unto my knowledge.

¹⁸For it is a pleasant thing if thou keep them within thee; they shall withal be fitted in thy lips.

¹⁹That thy trust may be in the LORD, I have made known to thee this day, even to thee.

²⁰Have not I written to thee excellent things in counsels and knowledge,

²¹That I might make thee know the certainty of the words of truth; that thou mightest answer the words of truth to them that send unto thee?

²²Rob not the poor, because he is poor: neither oppress the afflicted in the gate:

²³For the LORD will plead their cause, and spoil the soul of those that spoiled them.

²⁴Make no friendship with an angry man; and with a furious man thou shalt not go:

²⁵Lest thou learn his ways, and get a snare to thy soul.

²⁶Be not thou one of them that strike hands, or of them that are sureties for debts.

²⁷If thou hast nothing to pay, why should he take away thy bed from under thee?

²⁸Remove not the ancient landmark, which thy fathers have set.

²⁹Seest thou a man diligent in his business? he shall stand before kings; he shall not stand before mean men.

Wisdom Key

Because you've done it to me and it hurts, doesn't mean that I
have to do it back to you.

Today's Prayer

When our hearts receive scars, it is hard to feel beyond those hurts.
Father, I pray that You administer complete healing in my life and
in the lives of everyone in my family. Wash our minds clean of the
traumas of the past and instruct forgiveness to flow through our
spirits. Help us to see the benefits attached to forgiving and moving past yesterday into a tomorrow free of all bitterness and strife.

Q & A with Bishop George Bloomer

When intoxicated by the need to seek revenge against one's transgressor, how does an individual get sober long enough to reevaluate the situation with rationality and soundness of mind?

The question swings upon two hinges: intoxication and sobriety. When intoxicated, you're not in control of your emotions, thoughts, and actions. It is the consequences, many times, that sober us up. The Bible says, *"Be not drunk with wine wherein is excess"* (Ephesians 5:18). Wine in this context could be anything that intoxicates you: alcohol, sex, drugs, life's addictions, etc. The Bible says, *"Be sober, be vigilant; for your adversary the devil, as a roaring lion walketh about, seeking whom he may devour"* (1 Peter 5:8). The battle in life is to value those things that we consume, without becoming addicted and intoxicated by them. Sobriety is the balance. It becomes our equilibrium that keeps us grounded. Sober yourself with good thoughts. When you forgive a person, in all actuality, you're not forgiving the other individual, but rather, you're forgiving yourself.

Today's Positive Achievement

_____

_____

_____

_____

_____

_____

_____

_____

_____

_____

_____

_____

_____

_____

_____

_____

_____

_____

_____

_____

_____

_____

_____

Day Twenty-three

Proverbs 23

¹When thou sittest to eat with a ruler, consider diligently what is before thee: ²And put a knife to thy throat, if thou be a man given to appetite. ³Be not desirous of his dainties: for they are deceitful meat. ⁴Labour not to be rich: cease from thine own wisdom. ⁵Wilt thou set thine eyes upon that which is not? for riches certainly make themselves wings; they fly away as an eagle toward heaven. ⁶Eat thou not the bread of him that hath an evil eye, neither desire thou his dainty meats: ⁷For as he thinketh in his heart, so is he: Eat and drink, saith he to thee; but his heart is not with thee. ⁸The morsel which thou hast eaten shalt thou vomit up, and lose thy sweet words. ⁹Speak not in the ears of a fool: for he will despise the wisdom of thy words. ¹⁰Remove not the old landmark; and enter not into the fields of the fatherless: ¹¹For their redeemer is mighty; he shall plead their cause with thee. ¹²Apply thine heart unto instruction, and thine ears to the words of knowledge. ¹³Withhold not correction from the child: for if thou beatest him with the rod, he shall not die. ¹⁴Thou shalt beat him with the rod, and shalt deliver his soul from hell. ¹⁵My son, if thine heart be wise, my heart shall rejoice, even mine. ¹⁶Yea, my reins shall rejoice, when thy lips speak right things. ¹⁷Let not thine heart envy sinners: but be thou in the fear of the Lord all the day long. ¹⁸For surely there is an end; and thine expectation shall not be cut off. ¹⁹Hear thou, my son, and be wise, and guide thine heart in the way.

²⁰Be not among winebibbers; among riotous eaters of flesh: ²¹For the drunkard and the glutton shall come to poverty: and drowsiness shall clothe a man with rags. ²²Hearken unto thy father that begat thee, and despise not thy mother when she is old. ²³Buy the truth, and sell it not; also wisdom, and instruction, and understanding. ²⁴The father of the righteous shall greatly rejoice: and he that begetteth a wise child shall have joy of him. ²⁵Thy father and thy mother shall be glad, and she that bare thee shall rejoice. ²⁶My son, give me thine heart, and let thine eyes observe my ways. ²⁷For a whore is a deep ditch; and a strange woman is a narrow pit. ²⁸She also lieth in wait as for a prey, and increaseth the transgressors among men. ²⁹Who hath woe? who hath sorrow? who hath contentions? who hath babbling? who hath wounds without cause? who hath redness of eyes? ³⁰They that tarry long at the wine; they that go to seek mixed wine. ³¹Look not thou upon the wine when it is red, when it giveth his colour in the cup, when it moveth itself aright. ³²At the last it biteth like a serpent, and stingeth like an adder. ³³Thine eyes shall behold strange women, and thine heart shall utter perverse things. ³⁴Yea, thou shalt be as he that lieth down in the midst of the sea, or as he that lieth upon the top of a mast. ³⁵They have stricken me, shalt thou say, and I was not sick; they have beaten me, and I felt it not: when shall I awake? I will seek it yet again.

Wisdom Key

To measure the true intentions and integrity of people, watch what they say, and listen to how loud their actions speak.

Today's Prayer

God, give me discernment into myself and into the people around me. Help me to see the motivational factors driving me to act in ways that are detrimental to my walk with You. I want you to be proud of who I am becoming, and I want to rest soundly in the fact that I am becoming who You destined me to be. I choose to change and be a better person. Give me the wisdom to respect myself as Your creation, fearfully and wonderfully made for Your glory and pleasure.

Q & A with Bishop George Bloomer

When addiction comes to overtake entire families and the wisdom of God seems nowhere in sight, how is the unity and life of the family salvaged in order to get on a safe road to deliverance?

When an entire family structure is being steered by the addictive habits of one individual, the only safe road to deliverance is through and by the hand of God. You must be willing to make some "tough love" decisions in order to keep the addicted family member from destroying the entire family structure, while simultaneously keeping your ears tuned to the voice of God. Do not be moved by the emotional turbulence of the situation, but instead, know that even when it seems as if God is not talking, His voice is echoing the wisdom that you'll need to overcome every situation.

Today's Positive Achievement

Day Twenty-four

Proverbs 24

¹Be not thou envious against evil men, neither desire to be with them.

²For their heart studieth destruction, and their lips talk of mischief.

³Through wisdom is an house builded; and by understanding it is established:

⁴And by knowledge shall the chambers be filled with all precious and pleasant riches.

⁵A wise man is strong; yea, a man of knowledge increaseth strength.

⁶For by wise counsel thou shalt make thy war: and in multitude of counsellors there is safety.

⁷Wisdom is too high for a fool: he openeth not his mouth in the gate.

⁸He that deviseth to do evil shall be called a mischievous person.

⁹The thought of foolishness is sin: and the scorner is an abomination to men.

¹⁰If thou faint in the day of adversity, thy strength is small.

¹¹If thou forbear to deliver them that are drawn unto death, and those that are ready to be slain;

¹²If thou sayest, Behold, we knew it not; doth not he that pondereth the heart consider it? and he that keepeth thy soul, doth not he know it? and shall not he render to every man according to his works?

¹³My son, eat thou honey, because it is good; and the honeycomb, which is sweet to thy taste:

¹⁴So shall the knowledge of wisdom be unto thy soul: when thou hast found it, then there shall be a reward, and thy expectation shall not be cut off.

¹⁵Lay not wait, O wicked man, against the dwelling of the righteous; spoil not his resting place:

¹⁶For a just man falleth seven times, and riseth up again: but the wicked shall fall into mischief.

¹⁷Rejoice not when thine enemy falleth, and let not thine heart be glad when he stumbleth:

¹⁸Lest the LORD see it, and it displease him, and he turn away his wrath from him.

¹⁹Fret not thyself because of evil men, neither be thou envious at the wicked:

²⁰For there shall be no reward to the evil man; the candle of the wicked shall be put out.

²¹My son, fear thou the LORD and the king: and meddle not with them that are given to change:

²²For their calamity shall rise suddenly; and who knoweth the ruin of them both?

²³These things also belong to the wise. It is not good to have respect of persons in judgment.

²⁴He that saith unto the wicked, Thou are righteous; him shall the people curse, nations shall abhor him:

²⁵But to them that rebuke him shall be delight, and a good blessing shall come upon them.

²⁶Every man shall kiss his lips that giveth a right answer.

²⁷Prepare thy work without, and make it fit for thyself in the field; and afterwards build thine house.

²⁸Be not a witness against thy neighbour without cause; and deceive not with thy lips.

²⁹Say not, I will do so to him as he hath done to me: I will render to the man according to his work.

³⁰I went by the field of the slothful, and by the vineyard of the man void of understanding;

³¹And, lo, it was all grown over with thorns, and nettles had covered the face thereof, and the stone wall thereof was broken down.

³²Then I saw, and considered it well: I looked upon it, and received instruction.

³³Yet a little sleep, a little slumber, a little folding of the hands to sleep:

³⁴So shall thy poverty come as one that travelleth; and thy want as an armed man.

Wisdom Key

The greatest blessing you can look forward to tomorrow is hidden in how well you treat and bless your parents today.

Today's Prayer

Father, family is a sacred and holy blessing from You. Help me to honor and reverence my parents while I teach the next generation to respect and revere their elders. Help me to be diligent in every task I am given to do, and teach me to be a good steward over the things You have placed in my care. Give me strength for long, productive years, and help me to glorify You with each new day that comes my way. In good and bad times, let me be wise enough to lift the banner of praise to You, Father, for without You, I am nothing.

Q & A with Bishop George Bloomer

When the weight of being the one person who's holding an entire family together becomes too much to bear, how can an individual find relief without forsaking the family unit?

Through worship. In worship, there are wisdom answers. Holding together a family by yourself is impossible for one physical person to do continually. The strength that you pull from to do the impossible is from an anointing of God's supernatural wisdom and knowledge in order to hold it together. The pressure is coming from stress, lack of encouragement, and lack of recreation. There are two things that you ultimately must find time for in order to keep from losing who you are: worship and time for yourself.

Today's Positive Achievements

_____

_____

_____

_____

_____

_____

_____

_____

_____

_____

_____

_____

_____

_____

_____

_____

_____

_____

_____

_____

_____

_____

Day Twenty-five

Proverbs 25

[1]These are also proverbs of Solomon, which the men of Hezekiah king of Judah copied out.

[2]It is the glory of God to conceal a thing: but the honour of kings is to search out a matter.

[3]The heaven for height, and the earth for depth, and the heart of kings is unsearchable.

[4]Take away the dross from the silver, and there shall come forth a vessel for the finer.

[5]Take away the wicked from before the king, and his throne shall be established in righteousness.

[6]Put not forth thyself in the presence of the king, and stand not in the place of great men:

[7]For better it is that it be said unto thee, Come up hither; than that thou shouldest be put lower in the presence of the prince whom thine eyes have seen.

[8]Go not forth hastily to strive, lest thou know not what to do in the end thereof, when thy neighbour hath put thee to shame.

[9]Debate thy cause with thy neighbour himself; and discover not a secret to another:

[10]Lest he that heareth it put thee to shame, and thine infamy turn not away.

[11]A word fitly spoken is like apples of gold in pictures of silver.

[12]As an earring of gold, and an ornament of fine gold, so is a wise reprover upon an obedient ear.

[13]As the cold of snow in the time of harvest, so is a faithful messenger to them that send him: for he refresheth the soul of his masters.

[14]Whoso boasteth himself of a false gift is like clouds and wind without rain.

[15]By long forbearing is a prince persuaded, and a soft tongue breaketh the bone.

[16]Hast thou found honey? eat so much as is sufficient for thee, lest thou be filled therewith, and vomit it.

[17]Withdraw thy foot from thy neighbour's house; lest he be weary of thee, and so hate thee.

[18]A man that beareth false witness against his neighbour is a maul, and a sword, and a sharp arrow.

[19]Confidence in an unfaithful man in time of trouble is like a broken tooth, and a foot out of joint.

[20]As he that taketh away a garment in cold weather, and as vinegar upon nitre, so is he that singeth songs to an heavy heart.

[21]If thine enemy be hungry, give him bread to eat; and if he be thirsty, give him water to drink:

[22]For thou shalt heap coals of fire upon his head, and the LORD shall reward thee.

[23]The north wind driveth away rain: so doth an angry countenance a backbiting tongue.

[24]It is better to dwell in the corner of the housetop, than with a brawling woman and in a wide house.

[25]As cold waters to a thirsty soul, so is good news from a far country.

[26]A righteous man falling down before the wicked is as a troubled fountain, and a corrupt spring.

[27]It is not good to eat much honey: so for men to search their own glory is not glory.

[28]He that hath no rule over his own spirit is like a city that is broken down, and without walls.

Wisdom Key

The hardest decisions in life reveal the doorways to your greatest blessings.

Today's Prayer

Humility is a sensible attribute that each person needs in order to build a reputation of integrity. Lord, help me to see myself truthfully, so I can look at others through untainted eyes and conduct my life with honesty and decency. Help me to love myself, my neighbors, and my enemies. Teach me to always stay in a position of submission before You so my life and my steps can be ordered by You.

Q & A with Bishop George Bloomer

When making major, life-changing decisions, how do you determine whether or not you're being led by God or your own carnal desires?

This is habit-developing. When I develop a habit of acknowledging God in all my ways, then He opens doors and helps me to walk in. When I'm not acknowledging God, and I ask Him to help me in a situation after being saved for a number of years, while still doing things my own way, then chances are that the inner voice I hear is my flesh disguised as the voice of God. The only way you will know the voice of God is by entering into a pattern with Him of constantly asking Him those questions. And when you ask the Lord those questions, more and more, you'll become acquainted with His voice. That's how you know—by asking Him. God will speak through a growing awareness within, and open doors externally.

Today's Positive Achievement

_____

_____

_____

_____

_____

_____

_____

_____

_____

_____

_____

_____

_____

_____

_____

_____

_____

_____

_____

_____

_____

_____

Proverbs 26

[1] As snow in summer, and as rain in harvest, so honour is not seemly for a fool.

[2] As the bird by wandering, as the swallow by flying, so the curse causeless shall not come.

[3] A whip for the horse, a bridle for the ass, and a rod for the fool's back.

[4] Answer not a fool according to his folly, lest thou also be like unto him.

[5] Answer a fool according to his folly, lest he be wise in his own conceit.

[6] He that sendeth a message by the hand of a fool cutteth off the feet, and drinketh damage.

[7] The legs of the lame are not equal: so is a parable in the mouth of fools.

[8] As he that bindeth a stone in a sling, so is he that giveth honour to a fool.

[9] As a thorn goeth up into the hand of a drunkard, so is a parable in the mouths of fools.

[10] The great God that formed all things both rewardeth the fool, and rewardeth transgressors.

[11] As a dog returneth to his vomit, so a fool returneth to his folly.

[12] Seest thou a man wise in his own conceit? there is more hope of a fool than of him.

[13] The slothful man saith, There is a lion in the way; a lion is in the streets.

[14] As the door turneth upon his hinges, so doth the slothful upon his bed.

[15] The slothful hideth his hand in his bosom; it grieveth him to bring it again to his mouth.

[16] The sluggard is wiser in his own conceit than seven men that can render a reason.

[17] He that passeth by, and meddleth with strife belonging not to him, is like one that taketh a dog by the ears.

[18] As a mad man who casteth firebrands, arrows, and death,

[19] So is the man that deceiveth his neighbour, and saith, Am not I in sport?

[20] Where no wood is, there the fire goeth out: so where there is no talebearer, the strife ceaseth.

[21] As coals are to burning coals, and wood to fire; so is a contentious man to kindle strife.

[22] The words of a talebearer are as wounds, and they go down into the innermost parts of the belly.

[23] Burning lips and a wicked heart are like a potsherd covered with silver dross.

[24] He that hateth dissembleth with his lips, and layeth up deceit within him;

[25] When he speaketh fair, believe him not: for there are seven abominations in his heart.

[26] Whose hatred is covered by deceit, his wickedness shall be shewed before the whole congregation.

[27] Whoso diggeth a pit shall fall therein: and he that rolleth a stone, it will return upon him.

[28] A lying tongue hateth those that are afflicted by it; and a flattering mouth worketh ruin.

Wisdom Key

Sometimes saying "no" hurts. But in the end, it soothes a lifetime of pain.

Today's Prayer

Lord, please help me to learn from my mistakes. Help me to become the type of person who is reputed to be wise, sound, stable and secure. Help me to willingly consider and sensibly judge all constructive criticism. As I mature with each day, allow my hunger to learn from Your rebukes to continue as I fight to cultivate and expand my territory.

Q & A with Bishop George Bloomer

How should Christians conduct themselves when they are caught in a relationship with a hypocritical and gossiping person, from which they are unable to get out of?

Confrontation has always been very, very good because it's truthful. So the answer is, you confront the issues. When dealing with a person whose worship says one thing but character says another, that's never good. Our purpose in life is not only to befriend those people who are around us but to be a greater witness to the community. So confrontation is key. Be honest about the situation, tell them your distaste and your dislike, and move swiftly from them. That's wisdom.

Today's Positive Achievement

_____

_____

_____

_____

_____

_____

_____

_____

_____

_____

_____

_____

_____

_____

_____

_____

_____

_____

_____

_____

_____

_____

_____

Proverbs 27

¹Boast not thyself of to morrow; for thou knowest not what a day may bring forth.

²Let another man praise thee, and not thine own mouth; a stranger, and not thine own lips.

³A stone is heavy, and the sand weighty; but a fool's wrath is heavier than them both.

⁴Wrath is cruel, and anger is outrageous; but who is able to stand before envy?

⁵Open rebuke is better than secret love.

⁶Faithful are the wounds of a friend; but the kisses of an enemy are deceitful.

⁷The full soul loatheth an honeycomb; but to the hungry soul every bitter thing is sweet.

⁸As a bird that wandereth from her nest, so is a man that wandereth from his place.

⁹Ointment and perfume rejoice the heart: so doth the sweetness of a man's friend by hearty counsel.

¹⁰Thine own friend, and thy father's friend, forsake not; neither go into thy brother's house in the day of thy calamity: for better is a neighbour that is near than a brother far off.

¹¹My son, be wise, and make my heart glad, that I may answer him that reproacheth me.

¹²A prudent man foreseeth the evil, and hideth himself; but the simple pass on, and are punished.

¹³Take his garment that is surety for a stranger, and take a pledge of him for a strange woman.

¹⁴He that blesseth his friend with a loud voice, rising early in the morning, it shall be counted a curse to him.

¹⁵A continual dropping in a very rainy day and a contentious woman are alike.

¹⁶Whosoever hideth her hideth the wind, and the ointment of his right hand, which bewrayeth itself.

¹⁷Iron sharpeneth iron; so a man sharpeneth the countenance of his friend.

¹⁸Whoso keepeth the fig tree shall eat the fruit thereof: so he that waiteth on his master shall be honoured.

¹⁹As in water face answereth to face, so the heart of man to man.

²⁰Hell and destruction are never full; so the eyes of man are never satisfied.

²¹As the fining pot for silver, and the furnace for gold; so is a man to his praise.

²²Though thou shouldest bray a fool in a mortar among wheat with a pestle, yet will not his foolishness depart from him.

²³Be thou diligent to know the state of thy flocks, and look well to thy herds.

²⁴For riches are not for ever: and doth the crown endure to every generation?

²⁵The hay appeareth, and the tender grass sheweth itself, and herbs of the mountains are gathered.

²⁶The lambs are for thy clothing, and the goats are the price of the field.

²⁷And thou shalt have goats' milk enough for thy food, for the food of thy household, and for the maintenance for thy maidens.

Wisdom Key

Sometimes in order to attain great riches, you must help someone else to become wealthy first.

Today's Prayer

Generosity is the believer's savings account. Father, help me to let go of the wealth that You have given to me so that You can credit my heavenly bank account and trust me with more. I will store up my treasures in heaven by giving to needy people around me and by sowing into people and ministries that have sown into me.

Q & A with Bishop George Bloomer

How do you balance your giving?

I constantly flip back and forth between giving everything I have, even when I have bills to pay and responsibilities to take care of, and being too afraid to give anything at all. When people have questions about giving, many times it is due to condemnation they are feeling as a result of a sermon or a testimony they have heard. Out of that condemnation, they either give to be seen when they do not have the funds; or their hearts become contemptuous, and they refuse to give when they do have the means. The balance comes from the person's motive. *"For as the rain cometh down, and the snow from heaven, and returneth not thither, but watereth the earth, and maketh it bring forth and bud, that it may give seed to the sower, and bread to the eater"* (Isaiah 55:10). The Lord creates balance. It is not His intention or His will for you to eat your seed or sow your bread. Learn to distinguish between the two by seeking Him first in all things, and you will prosper.

Today's Positive Achievement

_____

_____

_____

_____

_____

_____

_____

_____

_____

_____

_____

_____

_____

_____

_____

_____

_____

_____

_____

_____

_____

_____

Day Twenty-eight

Proverbs 28

¹The wicked flee when no man pursueth: but the righteous are bold as a lion.

²For the transgression of a land many are the princes thereof: but by a man of understanding and knowledge the state thereof shall be prolonged.

³A poor man that oppresseth the poor is like a sweeping rain which leaveth no food.

⁴They that forsake the law praise the wicked: but such as keep the law contend with them.

⁵Evil men understand not judgment: but they that seek the Lord understand all things.

⁶Better is the poor that walketh in his uprightness, than he that is perverse in his ways, though he be rich.

⁷Whoso keepeth the law is a wise son: but he that is a companion of riotous men shameth his father.

⁸He that by usury and unjust gain increaseth his substance, he shall gather it for him that will pity the poor.

⁹He that turneth away his ear from hearing the law, even his prayer shall be abomination.

¹⁰Whoso causeth the righteous to go astray in an evil way, he shall fall himself into his own pit: but the upright shall have good things in possession.

¹¹The rich man is wise in his own conceit; but the poor that hath understanding searcheth him out.

¹²When righteous men do rejoice, there is great glory: but when the wicked rise, a man is hidden.

¹³He that covereth his sins shall not prosper: but whoso confesseth and forsaketh them shall have mercy.

¹⁴Happy is the man that feareth alway: but he that hardeneth his heart shall fall into mischief.

¹⁵As a roaring lion, and a ranging bear; so is a wicked ruler over the poor people.

¹⁶The prince that wanteth understanding is also a great oppressor: but he that hateth covetousness shall prolong his days.

¹⁷A man that doeth violence to the blood of any person shall flee to the pit; let no man stay him.

¹⁸Whoso walketh uprightly shall be saved: but he that is perverse in his ways shall fall at once.

¹⁹He that tilleth his land shall have plenty of bread: but he that followeth after vain persons shall have poverty enough.

²⁰A faithful man shall abound with blessings: but he that maketh haste to be rich shall not be innocent.

²¹To have respect of persons is not good: for for a piece of bread that man will transgress.

²²He that hasteth to be rich hath an evil eye, and considereth not that poverty shall come upon him.

²³He that rebuketh a man afterwards shall find more favour than he that flattereth with the tongue.

²⁴Whoso robbeth his father or his mother, and saith, It is no transgression; the same is the companion of a destroyer.

²⁵He that is of a proud heart stirreth up strife: but he that putteth his trust in the Lord shall be made fat.

²⁶He that trusteth in his own heart is a fool: but whoso walketh wisely, he shall be delivered.

²⁷He that giveth unto the poor shall not lack: but he that hideth his eyes shall have many a curse.

²⁸When the wicked rise, men hide themselves: but when they perish, the righteous increase.

Wisdom Key

Loneliness isn't always due to being alone. Sometimes it's due to self-deprivation of happiness.

Today's Prayer

Father, today help me to focus my eyes and my ears on You because You alone can see me through all the obstacles and trials of life. I believe that I am resting in the shadow of the Almighty, and I know as long as I stay in Your will and Your presence, I will be taken care of. Thank You for the wisdom You have given to me to know when to speak and when to be silent, when to move forward and when to be still and wait on You. You are my Redeemer and my Refuge. By Your stripes, I am healed and made whole.

Q & A with Bishop George Bloomer

When oppression and depression seem to dominate the mind, how does one break free long enough to seek the wisdom of God for an escape?

Through worship and praise. There's an old saying that goes, "Music has charms to soothe the savage breast." You must know how to set an atmosphere to free your mind from the cares of this world—sort of like the commercial, "Calgon, take me away." Don't allow the cares of this world to dominate your mind, but instead, always leave the path to God open through worship and praise.

Today's Positive Achievement

_____

_____

_____

_____

_____

_____

_____

_____

_____

_____

_____

_____

_____

_____

_____

_____

_____

_____

_____

_____

_____

_____

_____

Proverbs 29

¹He, that being often reproved hardeneth his neck, shall suddenly be destroyed, and that without remedy.

²When the righteous are in authority, the people rejoice: but when the wicked beareth rule, the people mourn.

³Whoso loveth wisdom rejoiceth his father: but he that keepeth company with harlots spendeth his substance.

⁴The king by judgment establisheth the land: but he that receiveth gifts overthroweth it.

⁵A man that flattereth his neighbour spreadeth a net for his feet.

⁶In the transgression of an evil man there is a snare: but the righteous doth sing and rejoice.

⁷The righteous considereth the cause of the poor: but the wicked regardeth not to know it.

⁸Scornful men bring a city into a snare: but wise men turn away wrath.

⁹If a wise man contendeth with a foolish man, whether he rage or laugh, there is no rest.

¹⁰The bloodthirsty hate the upright: but the just seek his soul.

¹¹A fool uttereth all his mind: but a wise man keepeth it in till afterwards.

¹²If a ruler hearken to lies, all his servants are wicked.

¹³The poor and the deceitful man meet together: the LORD lighteneth both their eyes.

¹⁴The king that faithfully judgeth the poor, his throne shall be established for ever.

¹⁵The rod and reproof give wisdom: but a child left to himself bringeth his mother to shame.

¹⁶When the wicked are multiplied, transgression increaseth: but the righteous shall see their fall.

¹⁷Correct thy son, and he shall give thee rest; yea, he shall give delight unto thy soul.

¹⁸Where there is no vision, the people perish: but he that keepeth the law, happy is he.

¹⁹A servant will not be corrected by words: for though he understand he will not answer.

²⁰Seest thou a man that is hasty in his words? there is more hope of a fool than of him.

²¹He that delicately bringeth up his servant from a child shall have him become his son at the length.

²²An angry man stirreth up strife, and a furious man aboundeth in transgression.

²³A man's pride shall bring him low: but honour shall uphold the humble in spirit.

²⁴Whoso is partner with a thief hateth his own soul: he heareth cursing, and bewrayeth it not.

²⁵The fear of man bringeth a snare: but whoso putteth his trust in the LORD shall be safe.

²⁶Many seek the ruler's favour; but every man's judgment cometh from the LORD.

²⁷An unjust man is an abomination to the just: and he that is upright in the way is abomination to the wicked.

Wisdom Key

Money comes to those who seek to help others and runs from those who seek to keep it.

Today's Prayer

Teach me to be wise. Help me to be shrewd in the decisions I make and the actions I take. I need more of Your understanding, insight, and knowledge to raise my family, operate in the business world, maneuver my investments, and walk blamelessly before You. Be with me, Father, and help me to glorify You as I exemplify that *"God hath chosen the foolish things of the world to confound the wise; and God hath chosen the weak things of the world to confound the things which are mighty"* (1 Corinthians 1:27).

Q & A with Bishop George Bloomer

For years my source of income has been working as a bartender in exclusive nightclubs. Now that I have received the Lord as my personal Savior, do I have to quit my job in order to remain saved?

You don't have to quit your job in order to remain saved. Salvation does not hinge upon that, but one would think that you would now need a change of environment and you wouldn't want to be the server of mind-altering and intoxicating beverages. The very reason for the question is that conviction has already set in for you. So you need to prayerfully seek the Lord for equal or better employment and I know the Lord is going to do better for you. Trust Him. He will guide you.

Today's Positive Achievement

_____

_____

_____

_____

_____

_____

_____

_____

_____

_____

_____

_____

_____

_____

_____

_____

_____

_____

_____

_____

_____

Day Thirty

Proverbs 30

¹The words of Agur the son of Jakeh, even the prophecy: the man spake unto Ithiel, even unto Ithiel and Ucal,
²Surely I am more brutish than any man, and have not the understanding of a man.
³I neither learned wisdom, nor have the knowledge of the holy.
⁴Who hath ascended up into heaven, or descended? who hath gathered the wind in his fists? who hath bound the waters in a garment? who hath established all the ends of the earth? what is his name, and what is his son's name, if thou canst tell?
⁵Every word of God is pure: he is a shield unto them that put their trust in him.
⁶Add thou not unto his words, lest he reprove thee, and thou be found a liar.
⁷Two things have I required of thee; deny me them not before I die:
⁸Remove far from me vanity and lies: give me neither poverty nor riches; feed me with food convenient for me:
⁹Lest I be full, and deny thee, and say, Who is the Lord? or lest I be poor, and steal, and take the name of my God in vain.
¹⁰Accuse not a servant unto his master, lest he curse thee, and thou be found guilty.
¹¹There is a generation that curseth their father, and doth not bless their mother.
¹²There is a generation that are pure in their own eyes, and yet is not washed from their filthiness.
¹³There is a generation, O how lofty are their eyes! and their eyelids are lifted up.
¹⁴There is a generation, whose teeth are as swords, and their jaw teeth as knives, to devour the poor from off the earth, and the needy from among men.
¹⁵The horseleach hath two daughters, crying, Give, give. There are three things that are never satisfied, yea, four things say not, It is enough:
¹⁶The grave; and the barren womb; the earth that is not filled with water; and the fire that saith not, It is enough.
¹⁷The eye that mocketh at his father, and despiseth to obey his mother, the ravens of the valley shall pick it out, and the young eagles shall eat it.
¹⁸There be three things which are too wonderful for me, yea, four which I know not:
¹⁹The way of an eagle in the air; the way of a serpent upon a rock; the way of a ship in the midst of the sea; and the way of a man with a maid.
²⁰Such is the way of an adulterous woman; she eateth, and wipeth her mouth, and saith, I have done no wickedness.
²¹For three things the earth is disquieted, and for four which it cannot bear:
²²For a servant when he reigneth; and a fool when he is filled with meat;
²³For an odious woman when she is married; and an handmaid that is heir to her mistress.
²⁴There be four things which are little upon the earth, but they are exceeding wise:
²⁵The ants are a people not strong, yet they prepare their meat in the summer;
²⁶The conies are but a feeble folk, yet make they their houses in the rocks;
²⁷The locusts have no king, yet go they forth all of them by bands;
²⁸The spider taketh hold with her hands, and is in kings' palaces.
²⁹There be three things which go well, yea, four are comely in going:
³⁰A lion which is strongest among beasts, and turneth not away for any;
³¹A greyhound; an he goat also; and a king, against whom there is no rising up.
³²If thou hast done foolishly in lifting up thyself, or if thou hast thought evil, lay thine hand upon thy mouth.
³³Surely the churning of milk bringeth forth butter, and the wringing of the nose bringeth forth blood: so the forcing of wrath bringeth forth strife.

Wisdom Key

Oppression causes wise men to make foolish mistakes, but a peaceful heart seeks the knowledge of God in all things.

Today's Prayer

Lord, I long to be content and satisfied in all things. Teach me to be thankful and grateful for every gift You give. Help me to stop looking on my neighbor's plate as I focus on my own soul salvation. Your will and Your plan are too big for me to ever comprehend or fathom, Father, so help me to trust that everything You do is perfect and just. Help me to know that the things I don't understand, You have complete control over. Help me to see that the omnipotent God I serve is more than capable of taking care of all things, no matter how big or small.

Q & A with Bishop George Bloomer

In dealing with grief, is it normal for an individual to spend months or years grieving, or does this type of prolonged grief constitute a need to seek therapy and counseling?

I don't want to suggest that I'm a medical doctor, or that I have studied grief or depression, because I haven't. What I will share with you are issues that have come out of my own counseling sessions and areas that I have dealt with personally. There is a time for grief and a period of grieving and mourning. In my experience, it shouldn't go on more than a month or two before you start moving back into some normalcy for your life that engages your usual routines. Sometimes the grieving process goes on longer than that, but there needs to be an effort on the part of those who are around to jolt you back into your normal pattern of life in order to keep you from dying with the person whose time and season are gone.

Remember, you're still here; so your season isn't up, and therefore, you must continue to exist without desiring to live in the hereafter now, but to live in the now, now.

Today's Positive Achievement

_____

_____

_____

_____

_____

_____

_____

_____

_____

_____

_____

_____

_____

_____

_____

_____

_____

_____

_____

_____

_____

Proverbs 31

¹The words of king Lemuel, the prophecy that his mother taught him. ²What, my son? and what, the son of my womb? and what, the son of my vows? ³Give not thy strength unto women, nor thy ways to that which destroyeth kings. ⁴It is not for kings, O Lemuel, it is not for kings to drink wine; nor for princes strong drink: ⁵Lest they drink, and forget the law, and pervert the judgment of any of the afflicted. ⁶Give strong drink unto him that is ready to perish, and wine unto those that be of heavy hearts. ⁷Let him drink, and forget his poverty, and remember his misery no more. ⁸Open thy mouth for the dumb in the cause of all such as are appointed to destruction. ⁹Open thy mouth, judge righteously, and plead the cause of the poor and needy. ¹⁰Who can find a virtuous woman? for her price is far above rubies. ¹¹The heart of her husband doth safely trust in her, so that he shall have no need of spoil. ¹²She will do him good and not evil all the days of her life. ¹³She seeketh wool, and flax, and worketh willingly with her hands. ¹⁴She is like the merchants' ships; she bringeth her food from afar. ¹⁵She riseth also while it is yet night, and giveth meat to her household, and a portion to her maidens. ¹⁶She considereth a field, and buyeth it: with the fruit of her hands she planteth a vineyard.

¹⁷She girdeth her loins with strength, and strengtheneth her arms. ¹⁸She perceiveth that her merchandise is good: her candle goeth not out by night. ¹⁹She layeth her hands to the spindle, and her hands hold the distaff. ²⁰She stretcheth out her hand to the poor; yea, she reacheth forth her hands to the needy. ²¹She is not afraid of the snow for her household: for all her household are clothed with scarlet. ²²She maketh herself coverings of tapestry; her clothing is silk and purple. ²³Her husband is known in the gates, when he sitteth among the elders of the land. ²⁴She maketh fine linen, and selleth it; and delivereth girdles unto the merchant. ²⁵Strength and honour are her clothing; and she shall rejoice in time to come. ²⁶She openeth her mouth with wisdom; and in her tongue is the law of kindness. ²⁷She looketh well to the ways of her household, and eateth not the bread of idleness. ²⁸Her children arise up, and call her blessed; her husband also, and he praiseth her. ²⁹Many daughters have done virtuously, but thou excellest them all. ³⁰Favour is deceitful, and beauty is vain: but a woman that feareth the Lord, she shall be praised. ³¹Give her of the fruit of her hands; and let her own works praise her in the gates.

Wisdom Key

The gift of life is a precious commodity. Treat each day as a gift you can't wait to unwrap to see what lies inside.

Today's Prayer

Wisdom, like a woman, is beautiful and graceful. Lord God, help me to have a life full of wisdom. Help me to pursue understanding like a bridegroom does his bride. Help me to nurture knowledge like a good wife does her family, and help me to rely upon discernment like an infant does his parents. I pray that wisdom overtakes me as I walk along this life path that You have ordained for me.

Q & A with Bishop George Bloomer

I have tried for so many years to become prosperous and to better my life financially, but continually seem to run against a brick wall. Where am I missing it and how do I change my situation?

There was a man who owned a cow. Not only was the man able to receive milk from the cow, but from the milk, he was also able to produce cheese and butter. One day, however, the owner decided he wanted a steak and killed the cow to satisfy his desire for meat. In essence, he killed his source of continual nourishment to satisfy a temporal desire. Soon after, the man starved to death. The cow was his source of nourishment, and because he killed his only source of sustenance, he destroyed all he had. It's cow management.

Look at your situation, and honestly ask yourself, "How am I not prosperous?" Prosperity means sustaining yourself through difficult times. Prosperity means constant growth. Chances are, you are prosperous, but you don't recognize the constant growth and climbing that is occurring in your life. You have not recognized or appreciated your prosperity. The wall that you are running into is your mind-set. You should never set your mind to think and believe that you are stuck in any situation. You must see the value in who you are, what you are accomplishing, and where God is growing you to. Appreciate your cow, and watch God give you steak.

But seek ye first the kingdom of God, and his righteousness; and all these things shall be added unto you.

(Matthew 6:33)

Today's Positive Achievement

_____

_____

_____

_____

_____

_____

_____

_____

_____

_____

_____

_____

_____

_____

_____

_____

_____

_____

_____

_____

_____

About the Author

Bishop George G. Bloomer is a native of Brooklyn, New York. After serving as an evangelist for fourteen years, Dr. Bloomer began pastoring in 1996. He is the founder and senior pastor of Bethel Family Worship Center in Durham, North Carolina, but continues to travel extensively, sharing with others his testimony of how the Lord delivered him from a life of poverty, drug abuse, sexual abuse, and mental anguish. "God had a plan for my life," Bloomer now says, "and even during my span of lawlessness, the angels of the Lord were protecting me because the call of God was upon my life."

Bloomer is the author of a number of books, including *More of Him*, *Authority Abusers*, and the national best seller, *Witchcraft in the Pews*. He has also collaborated with Mary K. Baxter on *A Divine Revelation of Deliverance*, *A Divine Revelation of Prayer*, and *A Divine Revelation of Healing*.

Bloomer is founder of Young Witnesses for Christ, a youth evangelistic outreach ministry with several chapters on college campuses throughout the United States, and bishop of C.L.U.R.T. (Come, Let Us Reason Together) International Assemblies, which includes over 80 churches nationwide and abroad. He conducts many seminars dealing with relationships, finances, and stress management. His message is one of deliverance and of a hope that far exceeds the desperation and oppression of many silent sufferers.